THE STORY OF
McLaren

Text and design copyright © 2025 Headline Publishing Group Limited

First published in 2025 by Welbeck
An Imprint of HEADLINE PUBLISHING GROUP

1

Apart from any use permitted under UK copyright law, this publication may only be reproduced, stored, or transmitted, in any form, or by any means, with prior permission in writing of the publishers or, in the case of reprographic production, in accordance with the terms of licences issued by the Copyright Licensing Agency.

Cataloguing in Publication Data is available from the British Library

Hardback ISBN 978-1-03542-396-5

Printed and bound in China

Headline's policy is to use papers that are natural, renewable and recyclable products and made from wood grown in well-managed forests and other controlled sources. The logging and manufacturing processes are expected to conform to the environmental regulations of the country of origin.

Disclaimer:
All trademarks, images, quotations, company names, registered names, products and logos used or cited in this book are the property of their respective owners and are used in this book for identification, review and editorial purposes only. This book is a publication of Headline Publishing Group Ltd and has not been licensed, approved, sponsored, or endorsed by any person or entity and has no connection or association to McLaren Automotive Limited.

HEADLINE PUBLISHING GROUP LIMITED
An Hachette UK Company
Carmelite House
50 Victoria Embankment
London EC4Y 0DZ

The authorised representative in the EEA is Hachette Ireland,
8 Castlecourt Centre, Dublin 15, D15 XTP3, Ireland (email: info@hbgi.ie)

www.headline.co.uk
www.hachette.co.uk

THE STORY OF
McLaren

A TRIBUTE TO AUTOMOTIVE EXCELLENCE

ALEX KALINAUCKAS

WELBECK

Contents

WHERE IT ALL BEGAN 06

MOVING ON 26

TRANSFORMING TIMES 44

AN ONGOING PROBLEM 62

WRITING LEGENDS 82

CLASH OF THE TITANS 102

A NEW START 120

TRANSFORMATION COMPLETE 140

INDEX 156

CREDITS 160

WHERE IT ALL BEGAN

THE GOOD GUY: BRUCE MCLAREN

"He was the most friendly and unassuming of all the Formula 1 circus."

Renowned motorsport magazine, *Autosport*, reflecting on Bruce McLaren – just two days after his death, aged 32. This story starts with his legend – one that encompassed 100 Grand Prix starts in Formula 1 motor racing, four of which ended in victory; his triumph at the famous 24 Hours of Le Mans sportscar race; and, of course, founding the organization that bears his name to this day. That he did it all with a friendly, humble reputation intact is one thing. That he achieved all that by age 29 is quite another.

OPPOSITE: The man who started it all: Bruce McLaren in 1965's French GP.

WHERE IT ALL BEGAN 9

Born in Auckland on 30 August 1937 to Les and Ruth, Bruce Leslie McLaren was raised in the Remuera suburb where his father ran a service station and garage. Contracting Perthes' disease aged nine put an end to Bruce's time captaining his school's junior rugby team. He spent months immobile having his legs set in plaster thanks to what were then the methods of treating the disease. It also left him with a left leg one-and-a-half inches shorter than his right (he would wear shoe lifts to compensate) and unable to play contact sports on medical advice.

He initially turned to rowing, but it was with his father's 1929 Ulster Austin Seven that his sporting aptitude returned and his engineering exploits flourished. Hillclimb success as a 15-year-old with a fresh driving licence was soon followed by saloon car racing and eventually his family purchasing a Cooper sportscar raced by Australian Formula 1 driver Jack Brabham. Bruce quickly began writing to Brabham in England, with the latter eventually suggesting he enter a pair of Cooper Formula 2 cars for them to race in the 1958 New Zealand Grand Prix. Gearbox trouble would mean Bruce did not see the chequered flag, but in coming second in the event's first heat race, he had done enough to win a bigger prize: the New Zealand International Grand Prix Association's 'Driver to Europe' scholarship. Two months later, Bruce flew to London – and his career began in earnest.

Upon his arrival in Britain, Bruce lived in a room in a pub near the Cooper factory. He would be racing the team's Formula 2 T45 car for the rest of the year. Success came quickly. During the 1958 German Grand Prix, which at the time permitted the smaller and slower Formula 2 cars to race alongside Formula 1 machinery on the monstrously long Nürburgring Nordschleife, Bruce finished first in class and fifth overall. This "made Bruce's name in Europe", according to acclaimed journalist and author, Doug Nye.

BELOW: Bruce racing a Cooper-Climax T45 Formula 2 car in the 1958 German GP, a race that forged his reputation in Europe soon after his arrival from New Zealand.

Bruce had sufficiently impressed Charles and John Cooper – father and son founders of the team for which Brabham already raced – for them to offer him regular Formula 1 race time alongside Brabham when they decided to concentrate solely on the top category for 1959.

His close bond with Brabham – Bruce would often visit Jack and his first wife, Betty, for Sunday lunch – shone through the season in which he would finish a creditable sixth in the drivers' world championship. His adaptability, consistency and eagerness to learn served him well as Brabham's understudy.

WHERE IT ALL BEGAN 11

OPPOSITE: Bruce's record-breaking first Formula 1 win came in the 1959 United States GP at Sebring – the race where his friend Jack Brabham clinched his first world title.

BELOW: Bruce and Jack Brabham shared a close bond – the pair are pictured here at the 1959 British GP at Aintree during their time as Cooper teammates.

Bruce scored his best result in the season-ending race at Sebring, Florida. With Brabham on the verge of clinching that year's world title, Bruce had dutifully followed behind early on. But when Brabham ran out of fuel, Bruce initially pulled over – agonizing over how to help his teammate. Brabham waved him on, and the Australian would eventually push his car over the line to seal fourth place and the title. Bruce, meanwhile, took the win. Aged 22, he became the youngest Formula 1 race winner – a record that stood for 64 years until Fernando Alonso's triumph in the 2003 Hungarian Grand Prix.

That victory brought considerable recognition, but Bruce's humble reputation showed no signs of changing – he just did not feel famous. Neither celebrity nor fortune drove him, instead he just wanted to enjoy working hard at motoring and motorsport.

WHERE IT ALL BEGAN 13

OPPOSITE: Bruce married Patty Broad in 1961. The pair are pictured here at the 1962 BRDC International Trophy meeting at Silverstone, where McLaren was racing for Cooper.

At the time, Bruce lived in a Surbiton bedsit near the Cooper factory, with his childhood friend and future McLaren Managing Director, Phil Kerr. The pair were often unable to afford all their meals, and while success and fame would follow in time, Nye recalled that "for the moment [Bruce] was utterly unspoiled, getting by on margarine" with the prospect of one day replacing it with butter.

Over the European winter of 1959–1960, Bruce returned to New Zealand. There he proposed to Patty Broad – the pair having met at a dance in early 1958. On his return to action for Cooper in Formula 1, he won the 1960 season Buenos Aires opener to double his victory tally. Brabham would ultimately dominate in 1960 to take a second successive title, with Bruce finishing second come the year's end. He failed to add any more wins for Cooper that year, but his impact was being felt elsewhere at the team.

In contrast to most racing drivers today, Bruce was adept at designing parts of the cars he raced. Having studied engineering at Auckland University of Technology, he would either have been a motor or civil engineer had his driving dream not worked out. In a sign of what was to come with his eponymous team – and harking back to the innovative efforts he had put into fixing the Austin Seven's engine – Bruce helped produce the 'Lowline Cooper'. This would race successfully in 1960, with Bruce even drawing some of the parts required when chief designer Owen Maddock was flat out. Brabham would win five successive races in the car.

In Bruce's personal life, things took another upward turn as Patty moved to England to work as a beautician. They married in Christchurch in 1961. Later that year, however, Cooper began to struggle with Formula 1's new engine rules, which required cars to be fitted with smaller, non-supercharged units.

BELOW: The 1964 Tasman Series, where the McLaren team began, was an eight-race championship across New Zealand and Australia eventually won by Bruce.

That year, the Cooper-Brabham partnership ended. Jack left to start his own team, which would take its founder to the 1966 Formula 1 world title. Charles Cooper was so upset by Brabham's decision – seeing it as a betrayal – that he initially tried to stop Bruce having any more influence on designing parts for the team's new-for-1962 car, the T60. Soon enough, however, Bruce's persistence with design suggestions, plus that ever-ready smile, won the Coopers over. He was able to contribute ideas once again with the new Type 60 car, which went on to win the 1962 Monaco Grand Prix. But that triumph would be Bruce's last in the world championship for over six years.

16 WHERE IT ALL BEGAN

Much of this was down to Cooper's decline as a Formula 1 powerhouse. The 1963 season was a disaster, with the team's T66 car proving unable to produce top results. Bruce began to feel frustrated at leading a struggling squad, but, smiling through adversity as he had done through the weeks and months of Perthes' disease treatment, 1963 would become a momentous year in his life. For it was as the season came to a close that Bruce founded McLaren. That too stemmed from his irritation with Cooper.

Bruce had wanted the team to enter a pair of specially designed cars for the new Tasman Series races that would kick off the 1964 motorsport season. Given the championship took place over four rounds in his native New Zealand and a further four races in Australia, Bruce was eager for success. But what he viewed as the Coopers' poor reaction to his suggestion convinced him that he should go it alone.

Across the final months of 1963, Bruce did a deal with Teddy Mayer – brother of rising American driving star, Timmy, who was set to join the Cooper team full-time for 1964 – to supply engines for the special Tasman Series cars. Bruce had decided he would build these without Cooper's assistance in the team's factory. They came together with Bruce's friend and mechanic – Wally Willmott – but it was Bruce's late 1963 alliance with the Mayers that would prove both terrific and tragic.

The Cooper F1-inspired cars produced by 'Bruce McLaren Motor Racing Ltd' were painted dark green, but with added 'Kiwi Silver' stripes. And they were fast. In the first Tasman race at the Levin track, Timmy Mayer finished second with Bruce third, while another New Zealander, Denny Hulme, won the race for Brabham's eponymous team. Next time out, Bruce triumphed in the 'New Zealand Grand Prix'. He won the next two races, but the McLaren cars struggled after heading to Australia. In the final round at Longford, Timmy Mayer was killed – his wayward car colliding with two trees in practice. McLaren was understandably subdued the next day, but nevertheless clinched the championship.

Heading back to Europe for the upcoming 1964 Formula 1 campaign with Cooper, as well as his sportscar exploits that included racing the famed Ford GT40 at Le Mans, Bruce's mind was made up.

"The die was cast," wrote Bruce's friend and later biographer, Eoin Young. "He'd proved he knew enough about racing to run his own team, which made racing exciting again."

Bruce viewed running his own team as a step above the goal his peers had previously viewed as the pinnacle of their careers: becoming a works driver for a team or automotive marque. As he wrote in one of his regular columns for *Autosport*: "now I enjoy nothing better than running my own cars again."

The McLaren project was still fledgling at this point – the squad's early years spent designing cars with a tiny crew. But a family spirit was imbued from the start, in large part thanks to Bruce being the same age or younger than many of his staff. They were all in it together.

Bruce's main job remained racing in Formula 1 for Cooper, plus his duties for Ford. The latter would prove to be pivotal in the story of McLaren's history. Alongside his Ford connection, Bruce earned his team a deal to compete in the 1965 Tasman series using Firestone tyres and then to test the company's racing rubber using McLaren's early single-seater prototype, the M2A.

"That contract plus Bruce's Ford involvement was instrumental in getting our company going," Mayer, by this stage McLaren team manager, would later say.

McLaren also did a did deal to produce designs for the Elva Cars marque and came to a profitable arrangement with Ford

OPPOSITE: Bruce's relationship with Ford helped the McLaren team, but his triumph here in the 1966 Le Mans 24 Hours for the marque burnished his racing reputation as well.

18 WHERE IT ALL BEGAN

to adapt GT40 sportscars. Bruce, meanwhile, worked on the single-seater design that would later become the famed M2B. This led to tensions with the Coopers, who feared the episode with Brabham was about to be repeated. That proved to be, as Bruce finally left Cooper at the end of 1965. McLaren had finished the M2B and was now about to enter motorsport's big-time.

In the year he would win Le Mans for Ford, Bruce's team took part in its first Formula 1 world championship race at the season-opening Monaco round. There, the M2B turned heads with its raucous engine noise before an oil leak and imminent engine failure put Bruce out. Despite his mounting major

racing achievements, however, Bruce had already realized there was a big problem.

McLaren had picked a Ford V8 engine to power the M2B that had originally been designed for use at the celebrated Indianapolis 500 oval race because Bruce and Mayer hoped the Ford organization would provide financial support to the new team. That was not to be, and the problematic engine was not used again until much later in 1966. In the meantime, McLaren tried out engines built by the Serenissima company, but these too proved troublesome.

The next year, Bruce opted to change his Formula 1 engine supplier – the first such instance in a long history of

BELOW: Bruce racing the first Formula 1 McLaren at the 1966 Monaco GP. The engine was not designed for the car, which attracted attention but proved problematic.

WHERE IT ALL BEGAN 21

McLaren engine power play. He picked the British Racing Motors marque that was adapting a powerful V12 engine from sportscar racing to use in 1967's M4B. But the engine was not ready until the final four rounds of that campaign, during which Bruce opted to enter three Formula 1 races for the Eagle team instead.

That same year, something important was happening elsewhere at McLaren. Having realized how lucrative sportscar races could be – even though they lacked Formula 1's glamour and fame – McLaren had decided to divert half its resources to the Canadian-American Challenge Cup sportscar series, where it had raced the M1B in the inaugural 1966 championship.

For 1967, the upgraded M6A – the first McLaren to feature a papaya orange colour scheme – made the difference and Bruce swept to the title with two wins. Hulme, meanwhile, won the first three rounds. He had signed to race for McLaren that year after much planning to join forces with Bruce.

Effectively, McLaren could fund its Formula 1 effort with its sportscar achievements – should they continue. Fuel sponsor fees and bonuses, plus selling older cars to privateer racers, also helped the team expand. But another critical choice was heading Bruce's way, one which transformed his team's reputation in Formula 1.

By 1967's end, Colin Chapman's Lotus squad had shown that the Ford-funded Cosworth DFV was the championship's best engine. And when Lotus' exclusivity arrangement concluded ahead of 1968, Bruce made sure his team bought in. The engines were expensive – £7,500 each – but produced 408bhp from a small, lightweight unit.

McLaren's 1968 M7A car made its Formula 1 world championship bow at the Spanish Grand Prix, where Bruce retired having spotted his fuel pressure running low and was unwilling to blow an expensive engine. Crashes and more

unreliability followed in Monaco before the breakthrough moment.

After Hulme led the early stages before retiring with engine damage, Bruce won the 1968 Belgian Grand Prix. He initially did not realize he had done so; Jackie Stewart having pitted from the lead ahead of him before the final lap at the long Spa-Francorchamps circuit.

Further McLaren Formula 1 success followed. Hulme won 1969's season-ending Mexican race – the year Bruce finished third in the drivers' standings after an experiment with a 4WD M9A design proved an expensive early failure. Can-Am continued to provide the cash, as Bruce won the 1969 championship, after Hulme's 1968 triumph had kept up the team's streak.

ABOVE: The 1968 Belgian GP was the McLaren team's first Formula 1 victory, but Bruce was only informed of his triumph in the paddock afterwards.

ABOVE: Bruce scored four Formula 1 wins before his death – three for Cooper between 1959–1962, where he is pictured here at Zandvoort, and one for McLaren.

OPPOSITE: Bruce was just 32 when he was killed. A missing pin for securing the M8D Can-Am's massive tail body meant this section was ripped off.

And so, 1970 started with McLaren on the up. Before a hammer blow fell.

Bruce was killed testing the M8D Can-Am car at the Goodwood testing track. The car's rear bodywork ripped off at high-speed and the resulting jolt to the rear wheels sent Bruce careering into a concrete-reinforced grass bank at over 100mph. There was no saving him.

"Too often in this demanding sport, unique in terms of ability, dedication, concentration and courage, someone pays a penalty for trying to do just that little bit better or go that little bit faster," said Sir Denis Blundell, quoting Bruce's own words on the death of double Formula 1 world champion Jim Clark in his *Autosport* column two years' prior.

The New Zealand High Commissioner was speaking at a memorial service at London's St Paul's Cathedral three weeks after the crash. Bruce had already been buried at St Mary's Cathedral in Auckland.

But McLaren would live on in Bruce's name.

WHERE IT ALL BEGAN 25

MOVING ON

THE BAD GUY: TEDDY MAYER

McLaren urgently needed a driver to replace Bruce on the racing front in Formula 1. And Teddy Mayer had finally worked out exactly what to do.

It'd taken a while. Shortly before Bruce's death, Denny Hulme had badly burned his hands in a practice fire ahead of the 1970 Indianapolis 500 – one of Mayer's chief projects as the burgeoning McLaren operation continued to split its interest between top level Formula 1 competition and lucrative American championships.

After the team had missed the 1970 Belgian GP in the aftermath of Bruce's demise and with Hulme absent, McLaren had blended youth with experience in its F1 cars. Four-time grand prix race winner Dan Gurney and rookie Peter Gethin appeared at the Dutch event, before Hulme reappeared in place of Gethin the next time out and the Englishman later replaced Gurney in turn.

OPPOSITE: Mayer and McLaren at the 1968 British GP at Brands Hatch.

MOVING ON 29

ABOVE: Eventual champion Denny Hulme races a McLaren M8D to victory in the 1970 Can-Am event at the Laguna Seca track in California.

Hulme managed to score three podium finishes on his return in 1970, but when he could not the following year, McLaren's points haul dropped significantly. Here, Mayer acted. He installed 1971 McLaren Indy 500 pole-winner Peter Revson to join Hulme. With the 1967 F1 world champion partnering a proven American open-wheel ace, McLaren's expectation in reviving its fortunes was set. Finally, it could move past the pain of Bruce's death.

Mayer had known Revson for well over a decade. With Mayer acting as team manager, Revson had driven for the Rev-Em Racing Team they formed with Timmy Mayer and Bill Smith – a successful businessman. Rev-Em Racing won 15 of 16 races in the 1962 USA Formula Junior championship, with Timmy's success earning an invitation to race for Ken Tyrrell – later a famous F1 team boss – in another Formula Junior series over in England the following year.

The Mayer brothers made the move across the Atlantic in mid-1963. They were from a wealthy family in Pennsylvania – where their father had been a stockbroker and their uncle a state governor. The brothers shared a passion for motorsport. Like Bruce, they'd started out racing an Austin-Healey, and from their first attempts in 1958 around Teddy's law studies, it quickly became clear that the younger Mayer, Timmy, was the superior driver. Teddy felt he was better in a management role anyway.

Teddy joined Timmy in travelling to join the Tyrrell Formula Junior team for three reasons. Aged 26 in 1963, the elder Mayer wanted to have a bit of a holiday and figure out his future career plans, but mainly he wanted to keep his brother company and

BELOW: Can-Am success – such as Peter Revson's here in 1971 at Laguna Seca – helped Mayer fund the McLaren organization while its Formula 1 operation struggled.

MOVING ON 31

BELOW: Denny Hulme's victory in the 1972 South African GP was McLaren's fifth overall in Formula 1, but was the team's first in three years and since Bruce's death. Hulme would score six McLaren F1 wins.

try to further his racing career. Soon enough, Bruce was visiting the Thames Island house where the Mayer brothers were living and planning the trip to the 1964 Tasman Series that would prove pivotal to the founding of McLaren – and would result in Timmy's tragic death in a crash at Longford.

Hit hard by his brother's death, Teddy returned to America. There, the keen skier carried on mulling his options. In the end, he concluded he could either make a go of being a motorsport team manager with Bruce or "go back to being a lawyer".

Bruce's initial response to Mayer's offer to run the fledgling McLaren operation was surprising – he felt Mayer should instead have a smaller role as a US-based team agent. But Mayer insisted and they soon came to an agreement. This had a significant financial element too, as Mayer invested in the team for a 50 per cent stake. Both McLaren owners were treating the team's initial years as rather speculative. Mayer still had his law

32 MOVING ON

degree and family money to fall back on, while Bruce at this stage remained a works Cooper driver.

"I wasn't particularly convinced that it would be an instant success and I certainly wasn't convinced that it was an excellent financial investment," Mayer would later say. "I didn't see it as a large loss either."

And so, Mayer returned to England in late spring 1964. McLaren was embryonic, with several of Bruce's friends working as mechanics. This, allied with its founder's endearing personality, would provide the strength of a familial bond. But Mayer felt it needed discipline too.

"In many ways he shook the tiny team rigid by taking it by the scruff of the neck, imposing discipline and forcing it to run with the accent on efficiency in all things," journalist Doug Nye assessed.

Mayer "hated time-wasters" and wanted McLaren operating with the order of an established manufacturer, even when its works at the time was a dirt-floored workshop in New Malden. He was forceful with suppliers – naturally establishing a 'Bad guy-Good guy' dynamic with Bruce. Nye called him a "short-fused martinet".

"We used the 'Bad Guy-Good Guy' thing occasionally, when it was right for the situation," Mayer explained. "It sure paid dividends too."

The pair complemented each other – Bruce's friendliness softening Mayer, and Teddy's directness hardening Bruce where required. But the arrival of a third key McLaren staffer meant Mayer would concentrate on the team's US ventures after all.

This was how Bruce's good friend Phil Kerr arrived as joint Managing Director in 1968, and it was he who'd be so key in convincing Hulme – another Kiwi – to race for McLaren that same year. Kerr handled most of McLaren's administrative

BELOW: Peter Revson would score two McLaren victories in Formula 1 and finish second in the team's M16 Indianapolis 500 car in 1971. He was killed in 1974 having joined Shadow.

work, then set the team's longer-term strategy and policy, with Teddy, after Bruce's death.

Before this, Teddy had made his mark on the company through the success of the Can-Am programme. With Kerr running the team's new factory in Colnbrook and its F1 efforts, Mayer and co followed the 1967 Can-Am title with a major deal with Gulf Oil for 1968 sponsorship. Another profitable agreement with US metals giant Reynolds followed. The success of the team in North America "kept us afloat and supported the F1 programme," Teddy said.

Gulf's colours would become closely associated with McLaren's Can-Am programme, where its successful 1967 car – the M6A – had become the team's first papaya orange machine. Mayer, inspired by a similar livery on a rival Lola car, had felt the bright colour really stood out on TV and in the mirrors of other cars. It would soon be synonymous with McLaren, as it was used on Bruce and Hulme's cars for the

team's first F1 and Indy 500 wins, plus many more designs.

The success of the M6A and its lineage meant McLaren's Can-Am streak lasted until 1971. Afterwards, its defeat to Penske-Porsche's turbocharged 917 car led to the team pulling out. Mayer felt engine turbo development "priced our kind of Can-Am out of existence". But success elsewhere in the USA soon followed.

McLaren's first entry to the Indy 500 had come because its post-1966 tyre supplier Goodyear had wanted to try and end rival Firestone's long run of success at the famed 500-mile race. But after Hulme's 1970 crash, McLaren's new-for-1971 M16 was a gamechanger.

The Offenhauser-engined car that had huge turbo lag and fearsome top speed finished second from pole in Revson's hands at the first attempt. Then Mark Donohue won in a privateer Penkse M16B the following year. Johnny Rutherford joined Revson for the 1973 running and he took pole too,

OPPOSITE: Emmerson Fittipaldi celebrates winning the 1974 Brazilian GP – his first for McLaren in the season he would go on to secure the team's first world titles.

before finishing ninth. But Rutherford was victorious in 1974 and 1976 for the McLaren works team – winning the race that provided a "purse of almost $1 million" to the winner, according to Nye. A big boost, after the Can-Am cash had gone.

Although McLaren took sporadic wins in American open-wheel racing to the end of the 1970s, as 1979 concluded the team decided to concentrate solely on F1. By that point, grand prix racing had finally taken over as the main source of the team's prize money income.

Not that things had been easy for Kerr's side of the organization, even with Revson aboard to partner Hulme for 1972 and some success following. In McLaren's M19s with markedly improved rear suspension, Hulme returned to the F1 podium first time out in Argentina, then won in South Africa – McLaren's first F1 win for nearly three years. Revson added three rostrum visits of his own to his teammate's final tally of six, as McLaren finished third in the constructors' championship. In 1973, Hulme triumphed in the Swedish GP, before Revson won twice – in Britain and Canada – and the team repeated its constructors' result from the previous year.

But even as F1's prize money offering was growing; financial pressure came from elsewhere. This was a period of rapid inflation in Britain, and by 1974 McLaren's sponsorship from the Yardley cosmetics company would no longer cover two cars (and the handful of one-off entries McLaren continued to provide).

Yardley was not happy, but the "impossible situation", as Mayer called it, eventually resulted in a deal being struck with Texaco and Marlboro – the latter, a cigarette industry giant, a new but major sponsorship player in F1 – for 1972 world champion Emerson Fittipaldi to replace Revson alongside Hulme for 1974. Yardley continued to sponsor a one-car team within McLaren that shared technical know-how, but raced the main cars competitively on-track for one year only.

MOVING ON 37

BELOW: James Hunt wins the 1976 Spanish GP at Jarama. Hunt was initially disqualified due to his car being deemed too wide, before McLaren successfully appealed two months later.

Hulme won 1974's season-opening round in Argentina, but Fittipaldi's home win in Brazil next time out and further triumphs in Belgium and Canada led to McLaren's biggest breakthrough: the F1 world title double.

But then the team changed comprehensively: Hulme retired from F1 and returned home to New Zealand, something Kerr soon did too. Mayer was therefore left "running the business on my own". And this meant he was in charge when one of McLaren's most revered F1 stories took place.

After finishing third in 1975 with two more wins, Fittipaldi abruptly decided to leave McLaren at the year's end. Mayer felt "we were left high and dry without a number one driver" for 1976. But with Teddy and co "on the phone to James Hunt whose Hesketh team had just recently folded, within minutes of putting the phone down on Emerson", and with Marlboro's blessing, McLaren felt it had a suitable replacement.

The 1976 season is one of F1's most famous. Fastidious Ferrari driver Niki Lauda – later a McLaren star too – dominated early on, while playboy Hunt grasped his chance at the big time as best he could.

Hunt won in Spain (after being initially disqualified on technical grounds before being reinstated) and France, plus was controversially disqualified from British GP victory for restarting following an early crash. Then, back at the fearsome Nürburgring, Lauda crashed and nearly died, while Hunt won. The British racer took another win in one of the two races Lauda missed before making a sensational return at Monza just six weeks after his crash, while two more Hunt wins meant they went into the Japan finale with Lauda just three points ahead (having been 34 in front before his crash).

In soaking conditions, Lauda withdrew citing safety concerns, while Hunt did enough to finish third around late

ABOVE: Teddy Mayer and James Hunt at the 1976 Japanese GP, where the latter sealed a famous drivers' world title with third place in a race that took place in treacherous wet conditions.

MOVING ON 39

OPPOSITE: Mayer and then-McLaren chief mechanic Gary Anderson with John Watson at the 1979 Italian GP at the Monza circuit.

puncture drama and claim McLaren's second drivers' world title. The team took second in the constructors', behind Ferrari.

Mayer said, "James was fantastic for us when he took his championship" and "good again the following year, once we got the M26 sorted out, but it all went bad for James and us in 1978".

That year McLaren struggled with its M26 car – even at one stage taking six different specifications of it to the British GP – and Hunt departed frustrated. Then "one hell of a blow" for Mayer followed, as the driver signed as his replacement, the highly rated Swede Ronnie Peterson, was killed in an horrendous accident at Monza almost as soon as the deal had been concluded.

Having dived down the F1 pecking order in 1978, McLaren could not pull itself up for 1979, even with a new ground-effect design inspired by the previously class-leading Lotus 79. Marlboro therefore brokered a deal with the Project 4 Formula 2 team – run by one Ron Dennis – which took effect in late 1980. That had been a season where McLaren fielded rising star Alain Prost as a rookie and popular British driver John Watson.

When Watson won his home race in McLaren's MP4/1 – one of the team's most famous F1 designs – Mayer "saw the future as quite bright". His feelings were only heightened when Lauda was coaxed out of early retirement to join McLaren for 1982.

But by this point the DFV was finally being overcome – mainly by the rise of turbo engines in F1. These expensive units worried Mayer, given his experience of soaring costs in Can-Am, but it was soon to be someone else's problem.

Mayer's shareholding in what was now McLaren International was bought out in late 1982, along with other smaller investors. With the team entering a new era, there was a new boss running the show.

40 MOVING ON

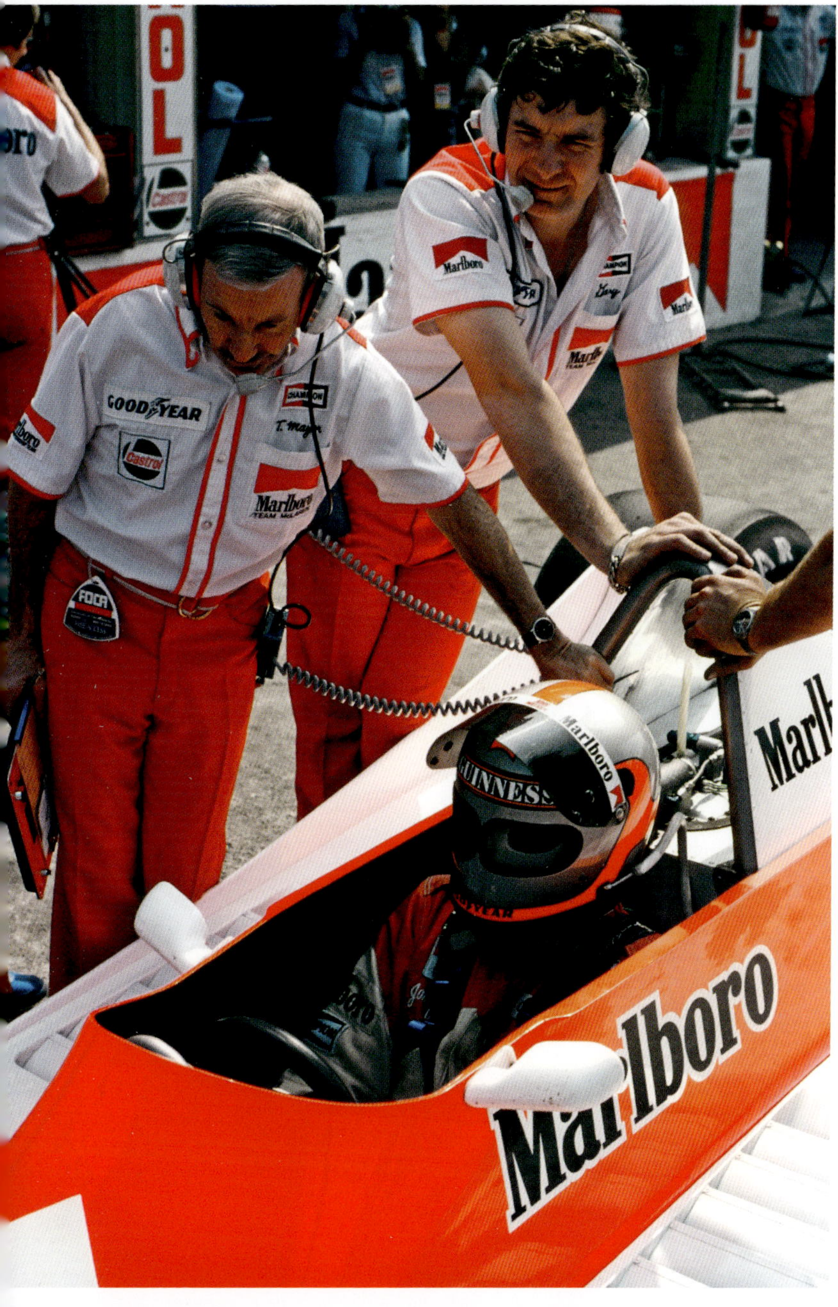
GOODYEAR
castrol
Marlboro
GUINNESS
Marlboro
Marlboro

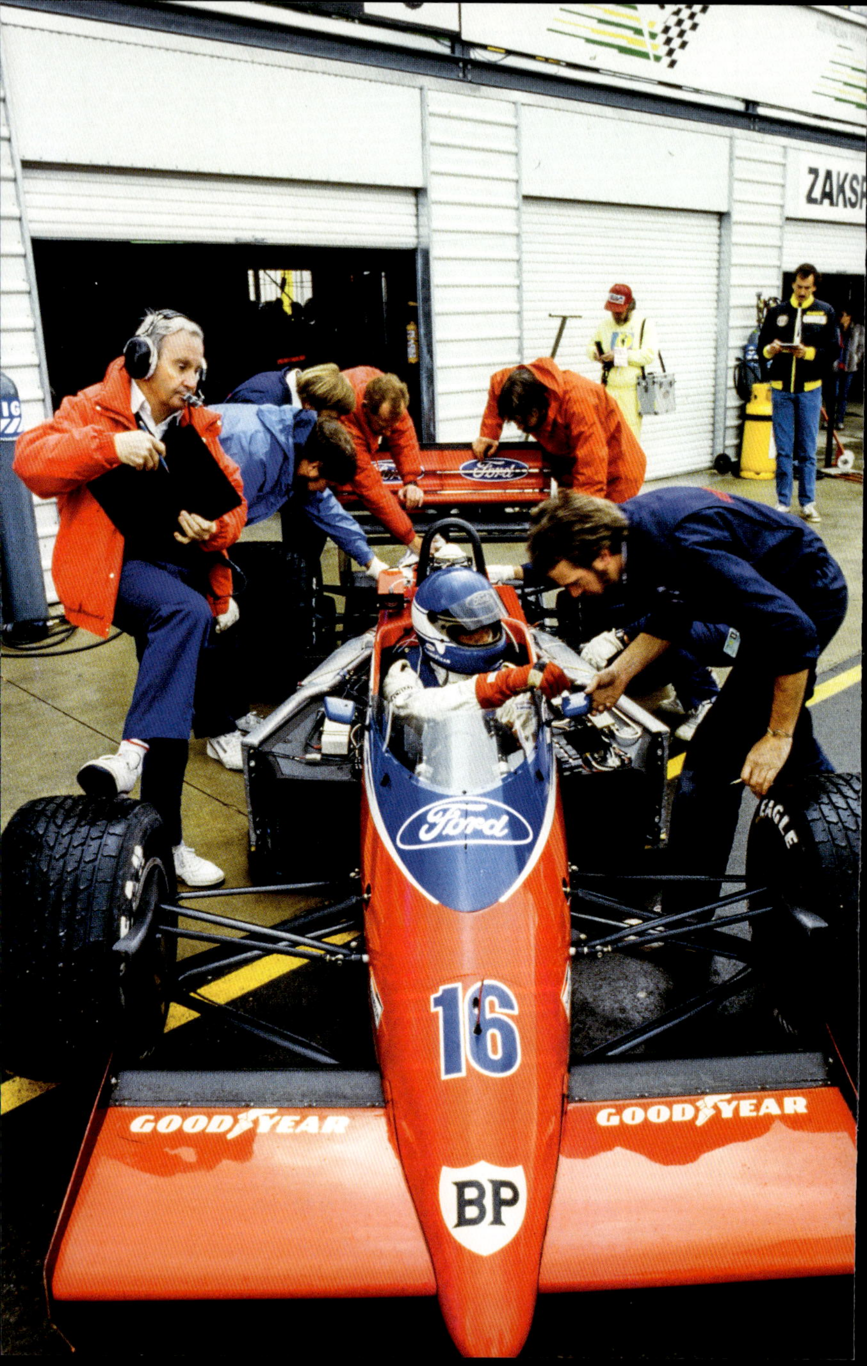
ZAKSP
Ford
Ford
16
GOODYEAR
GOODYEAR
BP
EAGLE

OPPOSITE: Mayer (left) here with Patrick Tambay's Haas-Lola in the pits at the 1986 Australian GP in Adelaide. Mayer was the short-lived squad's team manager.

RIGHT: Mayer and Dennis pictured here at the 1980 United States GP at Watkins Glen – shortly after McLaren's merger with the Project 4 organization.

MOVING ON 43

TRANSFORMING TIME

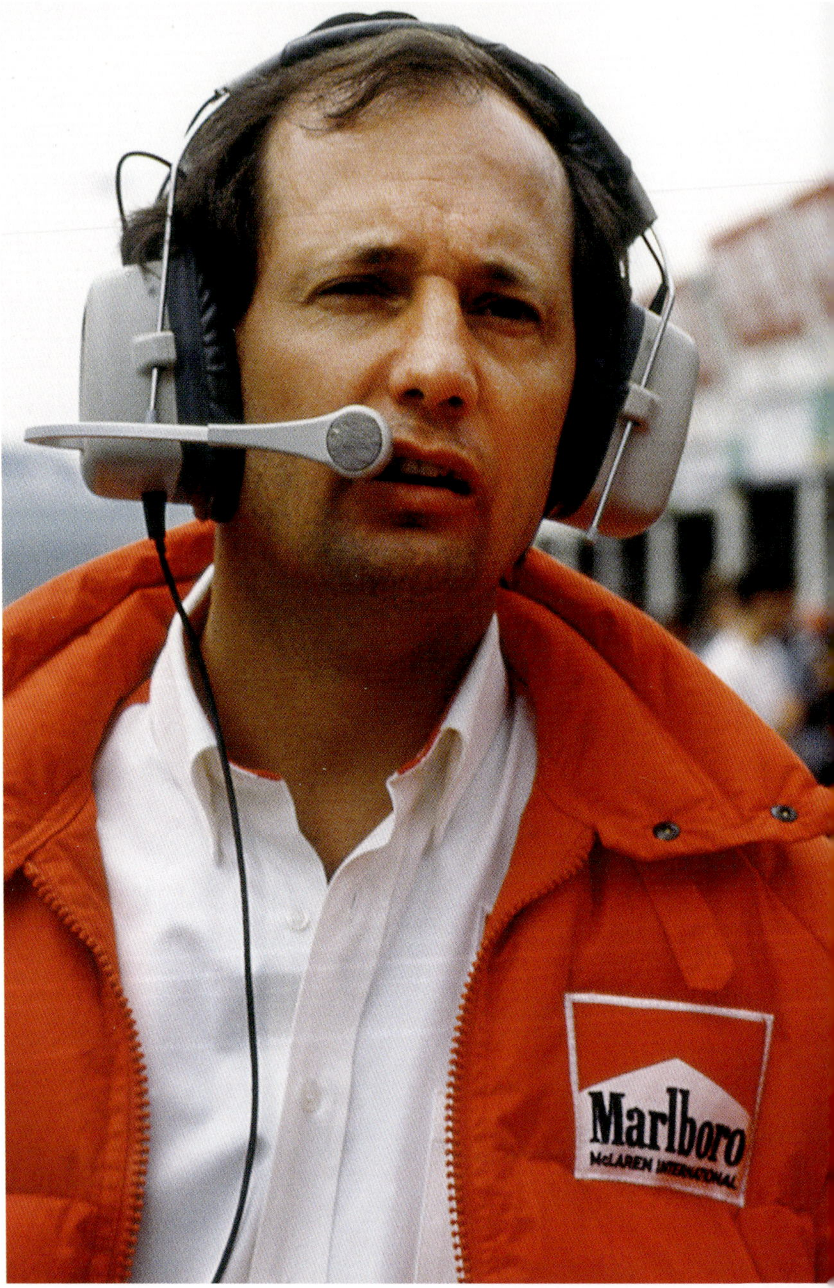
Marlboro
McLAREN INTERNATIONAL

THE BOSS: RON DENNIS

> "Staying solely and exclusively a Formula 1 team is almost surely going to lead to extinction. So, I think there is an imperative need to broaden the commercial basis of this company."

These words were uttered in March 2010. In the 30 years that followed Teddy Mayer's exit from McLaren, the team had secured 17 more F1 drivers' and constructors' world titles. And now McLaren was selling its own road-going supercars – a Ferrari with a British base, to some.

All of this had been achieved through the vision and drive of one man: Ron Dennis. No one, save for Bruce himself, can be said to have done more to establish McLaren as the organization it is today.

For Dennis took it from the team with recent memories of dirt-floor working to a major automotive player with F1 superteam status, boasting an enormous £300 million factory

OPPOSITE: Ron Dennis would helm McLaren for 36 years.

TRANSFORMING TIME 47

opened by Queen Elizabeth II. Dennis, as he outlined above, saw such a McLaren expansion as critical to its survival.

But so too was it vital for his own flourishing – ultimately into one of F1's most successful team bosses and a businessman trusted by the UK government to be an official business ambassador. Not bad for a man who had left school after taking his O-Levels and started out working for the Chipstead Motor Group. This organization came to own the Cooper F1 team when Bruce was still racing for it in 1965. Dennis himself, however, "positively bristles" at such condescending analysis – according to journalist Doug Nye.

"Perhaps because of that background, which is nothing to be ashamed of, he has always tried that bit harder to progress further," Nye continued.

Indeed, this explains much of what McLaren would become on his watch, as well as the way it set each new aim and strove to achieve them. For Dennis, it did not just matter that McLaren won in F1 or ultimately came to sell road cars, it was the manner in which it did so that was important. Shortly after Dennis took control of McLaren by buying out Mayer's shareholding, every team employee was issued with a company document that emphasized this point.

Something else prized fiercely by Dennis was cleanliness. For himself, but for his racing teams' facilities and products too.

"I truly believe that there's nothing clever about an organization which covers you in grease and sends you home stinking," he would say in the mid-1980s. "Striving for this perfection might sound trivial, but it makes for a better environment and certainly helps when we bring sponsors to the workshop. The standards apply right through the company."

Such an approach shone through his early ventures. By 1966, Dennis was working as a mechanic for Cooper in F1 aged just 18, before leaving to join the Brabham squad along with rising star driver Jochen Rindt for 1968. In the following two years, Dennis's efforts stood out to the point that Jack Brabham felt comfortable enough to leave him in charge of many elements of running the team – including cashing prize cheques and minding money required for F1 events while on the road.

As he lay by an Acapulco pool ahead of the 1970 F1 season finale in Mexico, Dennis came to think "why not do my own thing?" And so, for 1971, he did exactly that. He formed Rondel Racing with another ex-Brabham mechanic, Neil Trundle, which ran Brabham F2 cars in the European championship.

Rondel Racing's cars were "not particularly successful, although they were always impeccably, sparklingly prepared by

ABOVE: Dennis lifts the nose of Jochen Rindt's Cooper T81 at the 1966 Italian GP at Monza during his time working as a team mechanic.

TRANSFORMING TIME 49

BELOW: Hans-Joachim Stuck racing a BMW Procar at the Donington circuit in England for the Project 4 team that had built many of the championship's cars – an important element of its expansion.

Dennis and his men", according to Nye. But just as Dennis had begun to eye a graduation to F1 for 1974, the OAPEC Oil Crisis led to the team ceasing operations.

Here another man critical to McLaren's transformation enters the picture – Marlboro's John Hogan. He oversaw the company's motorsport sponsorship and advertising, and got Dennis to run what would become the Ecuador-Marlboro F2 team after Rondel Racing ended. But when that did not translate into quick success, Dennis was "determined to do my own thing again" from 1975. This became running more F2 machines in the European F2 series, under the banner "Project 3".

Dennis had come up with this name – he felt the practice of naming racing teams eponymously was best left behind – while lying in a bath this time. He viewed it as his third attempt at cracking the motorsport team management business. By 1976, his entity had become 'Project 4 Racing', which was securing interest from various motor racing sponsors – including Marlboro.

In 1979, Dennis partnered with former racing driver Creighton Brown – who would go on to become a McLaren board member – to form ICI Project Four, which ran a British Formula 3 team in addition to its F2 cars backed by Marlboro. The same year, Project 4 won a tender to build 15 cars for

ABOVE: Niki Lauda celebrates winning the 1982 United States GP West at Long Beach – his first victory for McLaren after Dennis convinced him to return to Formula 1. Lauda would score eight McLaren wins and the 1984 world title.

British teams competing in the new BMW ProCar M1 championship that would race on the F1 support bill featuring many star drivers. When Project 4 had completed its cars, the similarly aspirational Osella racing team had only done three of their 15 over in Italy. BMW subsequently got Dennis's organization to build ten more.

Marlboro then sponsored the team to take one of these cars racing, which it did with F1 legend Niki Lauda driving – before he entered self-imposed F1 retirement before the end of the 1979 season and concentrated on running his nascent airline. Lauda won the ProCar title, with Project 4 drivers also winning the 1979 and 1980 British F3 drivers' titles. So, reckoned Nye, "the only way forward was into Formula 1".

Part of how Dennis did this was to convince designer John Barnard to join his organization. Having sounded out successful F1 designers Gordon Murray of Brabham and Patrick Head of Williams, Barnard signed up having turned down an offer from Mayer to join McLaren first.

At the same time, McLaren biographer William Taylor claims Dennis and Marlboro – via Hogan – were already suggesting the two organizations merge. Mayer's squad was by this time in 1979 struggling, but he initially rejected the idea. Marlboro did not want to leave McLaren and its famous name and achievements, but the company also was not yet convinced Project 4 could do it alone. It nevertheless forced Mayer's hand, by threatening to drop McLaren's now critical sponsorship cash influx.

But, although an F1 innovator as famous as Lotus founder Colin Chapman did not think it was safe enough technology, Barnard had plans to revolutionize F1 car design in the MP4/1 – with an all-carbon fibre chassis.

BELOW: Niki Lauda racing in the 1983 Formula 1 season – the last year McLaren would run the Ford DFV engine before its successes were reignited with the TAG-Porsche power unit. Lauda pushed McLaren to test it in 1983.

TRANSFORMING TIME 53

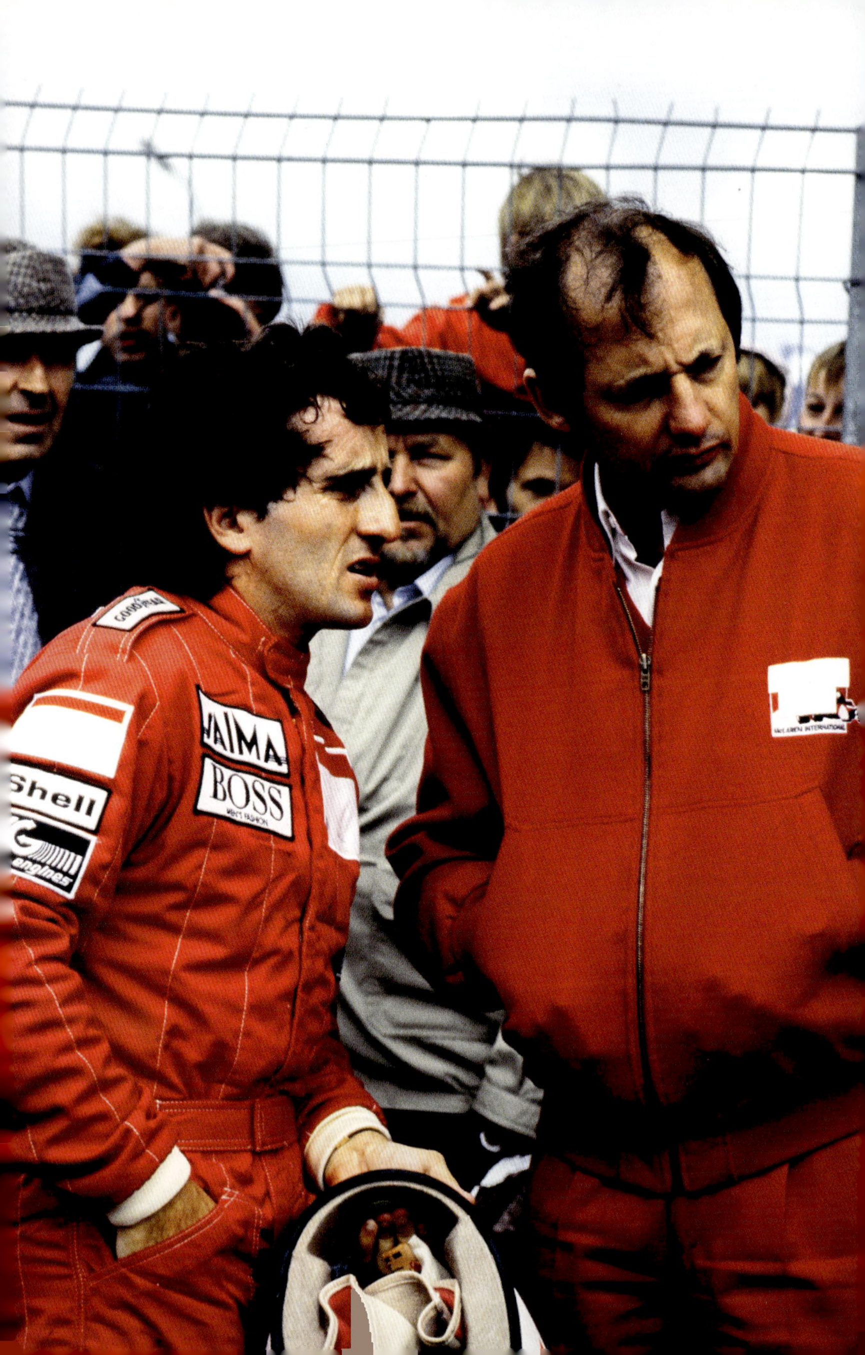
BOSS
Shell
engines

It was named after the Marlboro-brokered merger between the McLaren and Project 4 organizations that went through in November 1980. McLaren International was thus launched and, having worked together unofficially but to such a degree that McLaren's F1 results began to uptick by the end of 1980, the next year John Watson won the British GP in the MP4/1. This was imperative, as Marlboro had been promised that McLaren would win an F1 race for the first time since 1977 within a year of the union being completed.

Dennis, with his combative style and often needlessly expressive speaking manner, dubbed 'Ronspeak', was soon transforming McLaren. He secured what would become F1's best engine to replace the Ford DFV with the Techniques d'Avant Garde and Porsche organizations for 1984. In 1985, Dennis launched the McLaren Group to oversee the McLaren team, with TAG CEO Mansour Ojjeh as a co-owner, as well as of McLaren's additional subsidiary tech and engine companies.

Dennis's diplomacy and business nous were again on full display when he lured the surging might of Honda from Williams for 1988. At the same time, he had signed Ayrton Senna to race alongside Alain Prost and by this point McLaren had won 30 races under Dennis's control.

Prost had left McLaren after making his debut in 1980 to sign for Renault, before coming back to race alongside Lauda for 1984. Lauda, convinced of McLaren in part by his ProCar success and Dennis's subsequent attempts to convince him to race again, took the title that year, before Prost won the next two championships.

But Senna proved to be something else entirely. Dennis would later claim that Senna "saw the team was very competitive and made it very clear that he wanted to join".

OPPOSITE: Alain Prost (left), pictured at the German GP, returned to race for McLaren in 1984 after making his Formula 1 debut with the team in 1980.

TRANSFORMING TIME

ABOVE: Ayrton Senna on his way to winning the 1988 British GP at Silverstone for McLaren – a race in which Alain Prost decided to park the other MP4-4.

OPPOSITE: Ayrton Senna and Alain Prost walk from their crash at the start of the 1990 Japanese GP, which the former controversially triggered, sealing his second world title.

Dennis also revealed how Senna's "pretty healthy appetite for money" meant they "started to butt heads on money, half a million, and couldn't agree and this got really tense – it was becoming relationship-threatening". At Dennis's suggestion, the result of a coin-flip for what would become Senna's first three-year contract with McLaren – worth $1.5million – "was the only way to break our log jam".

Once that was settled, Senna then immediately made good on his junior and early F1 career promise by winning the 1988 world title – during which Prost blamed Senna for breaking agreements on in-race battling (Dennis felt it went both ways and that each also secretly lobbied Honda for better engines).

In 1989, the ever-rising tensions led to Prost deciding to join Ferrari for 1990, with the controversial fallout from the Japanese GP crash and Senna's subsequent disqualification

TRANSFORMING TIME 57

ABOVE: Ayrton Senna struggles to hoist the winner's trophy at his home race in Brazil in 1991. He'd suffered muscle spasms while battling a gearbox problem.

leading to McLaren appealing a result that had made one of its own drivers (Prost) world champion again.

For this really was Senna's team now, and although the 1989 result was upheld, he would go on to dominate F1 for McLaren with the 1990 and 1991 world title doubles. Dennis reflected that these results meant by now he felt compelled to "raise my game" on the management front too. Up to this stage, McLaren had won 69 races and 13 championships under Dennis's stewardship. But trouble was ahead.

First, Honda lost its place as F1's best engine, and then Williams's active suspension innovations in 1992 led it to become the championship's top team once again. At the same

58 TRANSFORMING TIME

time, McLaren was pressing ahead with its F1 road car project.

Barnard had been replaced by Murray to head McLaren's design team ahead of 1987, but although it carried on its success drive through the early Honda years, the development of the F1 road car – under Murray's design watch – led to some observers wondering if McLaren's expanding focus would come at a cost to its F1 results.

With these diving anyway as the end of the Honda era approached in 1992, Senna began feeling frustrated.

McLaren having to run a customer Ford engine for 1993 to replace the effective works arrangement it'd had with Honda caused him concern. So too did Prost returning to F1 with Williams that year following a sabbatical and winning

BELOW: Dennis with Norbert Haug (right), the man in charge of Mercedes' motorsport activities. The German automotive giant joined forces with McLaren for the 1995 season.

TRANSFORMING TIME 59

BELOW: Dennis with Ayrton Senna in early 1994, after the Brazilian driver had made his ill-fated move to join Williams following six years and 35 wins for McLaren.

a championship Senna had led after the one-third mark due to some of his best F1 career victories. That McLaren's funds were restricted by having to pay for the Ford engines only added to Senna's gripes, as this had a knock-on effect on his salary negotiations, as his contract had run out at the end of 1992.

Senna ultimately only confirmed he would be racing for McLaren in 1993 after entering into a deal that worked out at $1 million a race over the 16-event season. He also only agreed to turn up if the money arrived in his bank account in the days leading up to each respective race. Having been left feeling like his time with the team was effectively over – a feeling compounded by Honda's withdrawal in 1992 – Senna spent early 1993 planning what would become his ultimately tragic move to Williams for 1994.

"In 24-and-a-half years I was at McLaren we were profitable in F1 and our other businesses every single year apart from 1992–93," Dennis's protégé, Martin Whitmarsh, would be quoted saying by *Autosport* in 2021. "When we lost £1.5million and we were paying Ayrton a million dollars a race…"

Dennis had a plan in place, should Senna not return to race in 1993 – or indeed if he missed one of his $1 million races. He had signed highly rated young Lotus driver Mika Häkkinen to act as either a race or test driver, with Häkkinen eventually being installed as Senna's final McLaren teammate. This was because McLaren dropped the underperforming Michael Andretti before 1993's end.

Senna left McLaren for the 1994 season but would die during just his third race for Williams. Dennis was left devastated.

But as he dealt with his grief, he also had a serious task to complete for McLaren – solving something of a recurring problem in the team's history with F1 engine supplies.

ABOVE:
Formula 1 drivers including Alain Prost and Jackie Stewart (right centre) gather for Ayrton Senna's funeral in Sao Paulo in May 1994.

AN ONGOING
PROBLEM

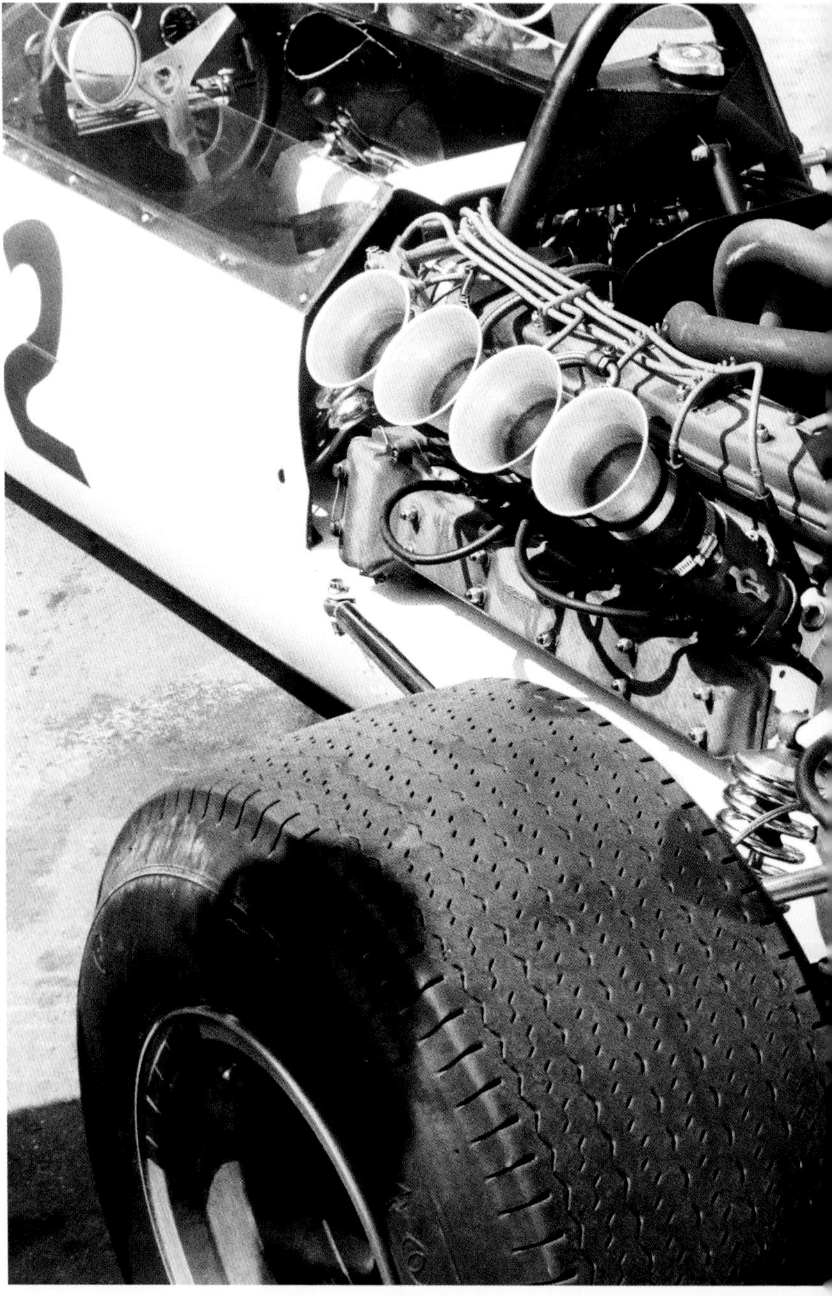

THE POWER:
ENGINES

There is a word in Formula 1's complex and ever-expanding lexicon that encompasses the McLaren story to this point: *'garagistes'*.

It's a term coined by Enzo Ferrari – eponymous titan of motor racing and luxury car selling. Enzo used it to describe the upstart privateer teams that challenged his established manufacturer for Formula 1 supremacy in the world championship's infancy – how they built cars with fewer resources, smaller factories, often without providing production models. It was not a compliment.

McLaren's early glories from Bruce's vision and Teddy Mayer's management were undoubted garagiste successes. How Ron Dennis transformed McLaren into a motoring powerhouse that now rivals Ferrari in the supercar automotive business, all while collecting world titles and building a factory as grand as that in Maranello, shows how the organization grew clear of Enzo's scorn.

OPPOSITE: McLaren's first Formula 1 car with its adapted Ford V8 engine.

BELOW: By McLaren's second Formula 1 race in 1966, here at Spa-Francorchamps in Belgium, Bruce had decided to trial a Serenissima engine.

But linking all of McLaren's growth together is the need for power. Specifically, engine power.

Garagiste F1 squads inevitably had to buy in the products of other manufacturers, which they might tune to their own preferences. But Dennis turned McLaren into a quasi-works operation in the championship, which had the best engines provided by companies seeking a different sort of motorsport glory. Today, it has fallen into a different realm – that of an engine customer squad tied to the strengths and weaknesses of a supplier, without much influence on squeezing extra power within F1's restrictive rules requirements.

After BMW supplied the V12 engine used in the McLaren F1 road car, the Ricardo engineering company has helped McLaren create all the power units on its supercar fleet ever since. In F1, however, nine engine builders have had their products placed in the back of McLaren machines. Of the current grid, only Williams has had a wider spread of engine suppliers.

Bruce's first F1 McLaren struggled with its Ford V8 engine in three races across 1966. Fast forward another 27 years, McLaren's MP4/8 – the last McLaren Ayrton Senna ever drove – was powered by another Ford V8. The team had signed up with Ford after Honda had departed F1 in 1992, but as it would run engines a development specification behind those used at Benetton (where Ford already had an existing contract) the deal was not viewed as a long-term prospect.

Before this, the Ford Cosworth DFV Bruce had finally been able to fit in 1968 powered 30 McLaren F1 wins – and was

BELOW: Denny Hulme, second, in action at the 1968 South African GP – the last Formula 1 event in which McLaren would race with a BRM engine.

AN ONGOING PROBLEM 67

ABOVE: A Lotus 49 from the 1967 Formula 1 season. The British team held an exclusivity agreement to run the Ford Cosworth DFV engine that year.

fitted to the M23 cars that Emerson Fittipaldi and James Hunt took to their world titles. The Nicholson McLaren Engines company (co-founded by McLaren in 1972) tuned the DFVs in these cars to extract more power.

Serenissima and BRM powered McLarens for three and seven F1 events respectively in the team's first two seasons. In 1970, Italian racers Andrea de Adamich and Nanni Galli raced McLarens that were fitted with Alfa Romeo engines after the Italian manufacturer eyed an F1 return and did this toe-dipping deal for its factory drivers. But after it did not yield any notable results (de Adamich failed to qualify five times) it was not repeated.

68 AN ONGOING PROBLEM

As Mayer's time running McLaren was ending in 1982, it was becoming clear that turbo engines were going to revolutionize F1. Knowing from his Can-Am experience that this would inflate costs, Mayer cast around for alternatives before he left McLaren. Renault, BMW, various Formula 2 engine builders – all were considered but declared not viable for team designer John Barnard.

It was Dennis who suggested an alternative – a decision that would prove pivotal in his quest to transform McLaren – in Porsche. The very company whose turbos had ended McLaren's Can-Am success story.

After a rapidly arranged meeting at Porsche's Weissach factory, McLaren had found a willing partner for its first turbo F1 project. But there was a problem. At this stage, the team could only afford to pay for the research and development of what would become the new TTE PO1 V6 turbo engine, but not the building and running supply of the race varieties.

BELOW: Emerson Fittipaldi in action during the 1974 Monaco GP for McLaren – racing the team's M23 car with its Ford Cosworth DFV engine.

AN ONGOING PROBLEM 69

Dennis had another plan, however. In the six months of 1983 Porsche would need for development, he would find the required funding to go racing. The eventual solution was already involved in F1 – sponsoring Williams during its world title run between 1980–1981. This was Techniques d'Avant Garde (TAG) and its CEO Mansour Ojjeh.

McLaren gained valuable insight from racing development TTE PO1s in a car for which the engine had not been designed in 1983 – the E iteration of the MP4/1 – after Niki Lauda agitated for such useful race testing. Barnard had been reluctant, but after McLaren discovered it needed to develop better braking technology alongside the additional power coming from the new engine or waste its potential, hopes were high for the start of the TAG-Porsche engine era the following year.

Things remained complicated as the new championship commenced, however.

Alain Prost – now re-signed with the team for which he had made his F1 debut – had his MP4/2 car built on-site at the Brazil season opener. Despite the late-hour car build, Prost won after Lauda had retired from the lead due to an electrical gremlin occurring.

Come the season's end, Lauda beat Prost to the title by just half a point (as half-points had to be awarded at the shortened, rain-affected Monaco GP). To date, this remains the closest points difference between the top two drivers in the world championship's history. Another two titles would follow for McLaren in 1985 – after which Lauda retired – and 1986. Both went to Prost.

Ultimately, McLaren would take the TAG-Porsche power to constructors' titles in 1984 and 1985, with the engine's race victory total hitting 25.

OPPOSITE: Alain Prost on his way to winning the 1984 Monaco GP. The shortened race meant only half-points were awarded – critical to Prost's eventual championship defeat.

70 AN ONGOING PROBLEM

andy
DOMESTIC APPLIANCES
Marlboro
SAIMA
7
Marlboro
Marlboro

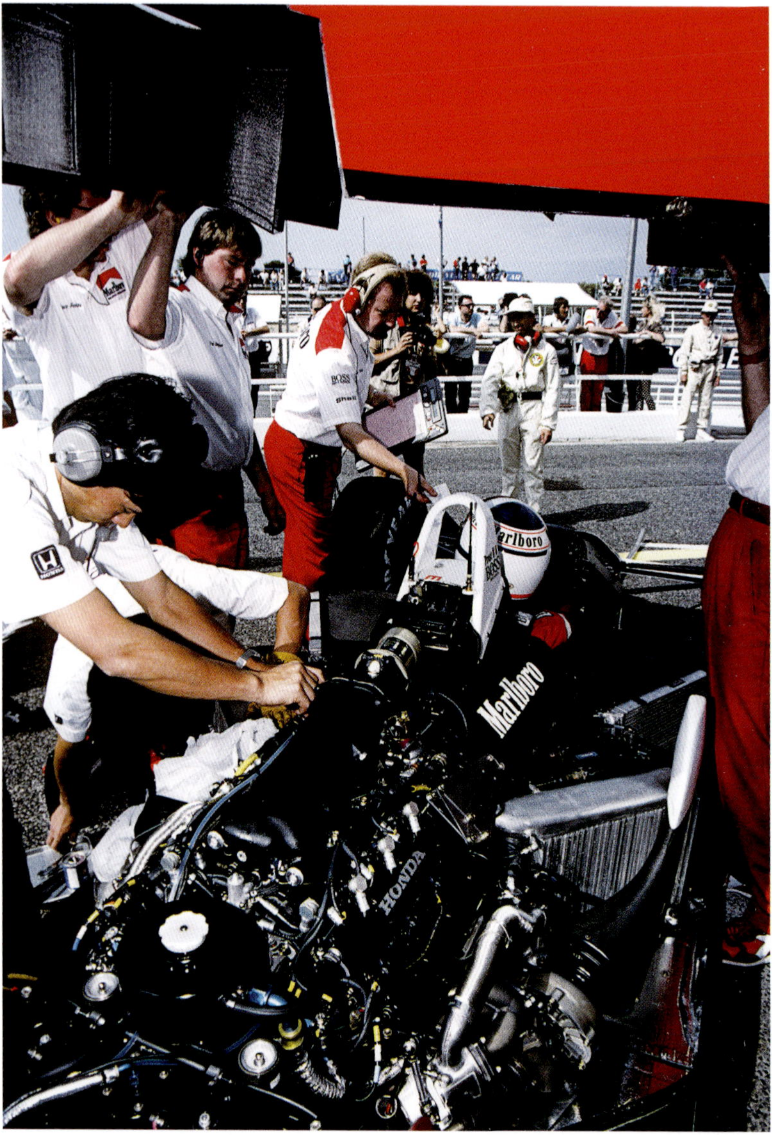
Marlboro
Marlboro
HONDA

But in 1987, Honda had powered Williams back to full double title success in F1 with its own 1.5-litre turbo engine (the naturally aspirated engines at other teams were typically 3.5-litre V8s during this period) after the team had clinched the 1986 constructors' title ahead of McLaren. At the same time, Honda had begun supplying the Lotus team for which Senna was now turning heads. In a mark of his famed shrewdness, the Brazilian had formed close ties with Honda engineers and managers.

Dennis could see all this, while at the same time having to plan ahead around a big upcoming F1 rule change – a return to normally aspirated engines for 1989. In 1988, he tied it all together and created one of F1's first 'superteams'.

Although he already had a double world champion in Prost, Dennis brought in Senna to form their famous partnership. At the same time, he snared Honda from Williams – benefiting from his efforts to learn and understand Japanese management practices to impress the manufacturer's executives. This all combined in a new McLaren factory in Woking business park.

In 1988, despite rule changes aimed at making things harder for turbo-powered cars, Honda's all-new RA168E dominated. Although Lotus had it too, McLaren took 15 from 16 possible wins and Senna clinched his first world title immediately with his new team.

For 1989, Honda's first naturally aspirated V10 – a 3.5-litre engine – again powered McLaren to the F1 world titles. This controversially went to Prost on the drivers' side, as the tension-filled Senna partnership exploded spectacularly at that season's Japanese GP. Things also were not as straightforward in terms of the MP4/5's engine reliability, but Dennis made sure not to criticize Honda in public.

OPPOSITE: Although it was only used by McLaren for one season, Honda's RA168E 1.5 V6 turbo engine went down in Formula 1 history, powering the MP4-4 to 15 wins.

OVERLEAF: During McLaren's one season back using Ford engine power in 1993, Ayrton Senna scored five Formula 1 wins, which are considered amongst his best in the championship.

AN ONGOING PROBLEM 73

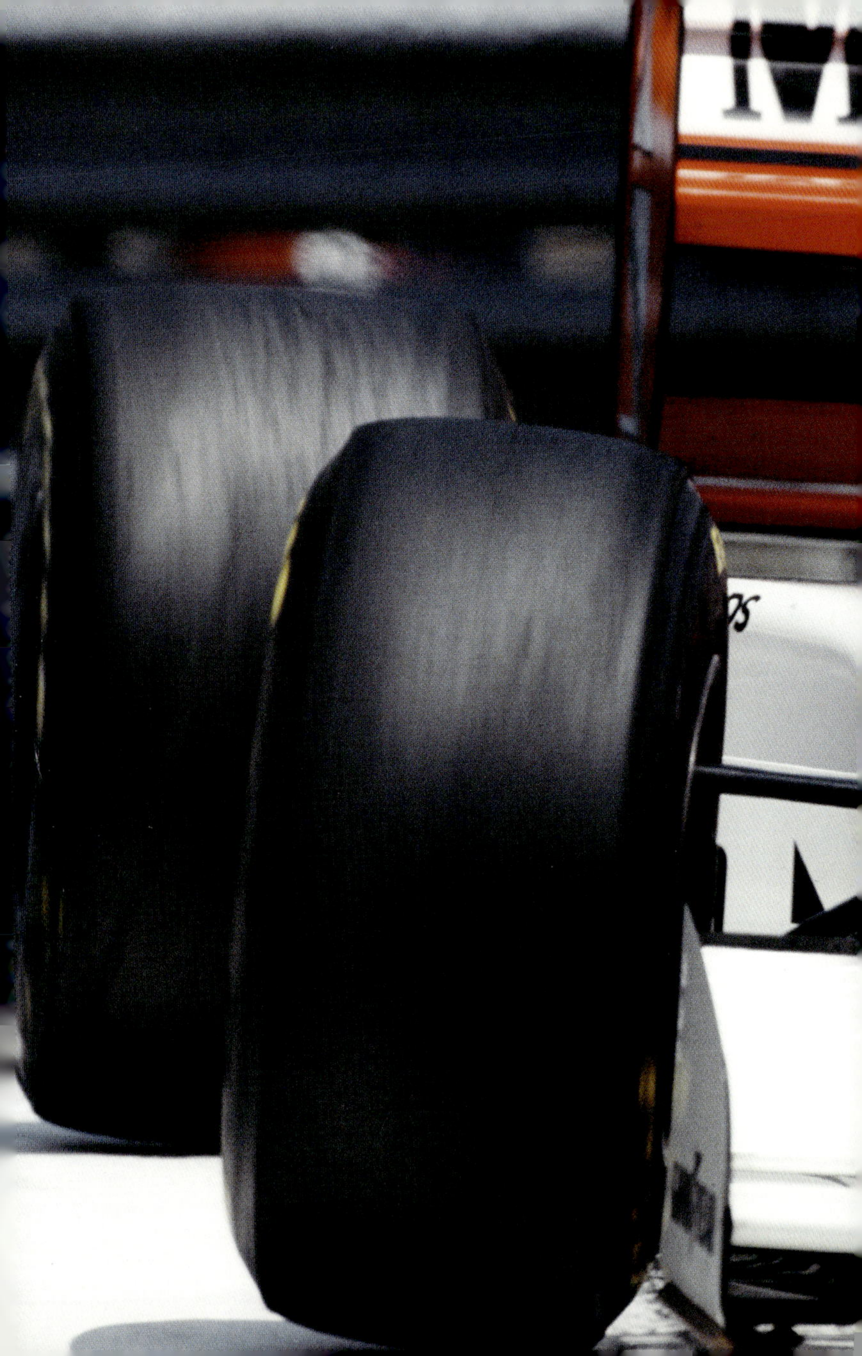

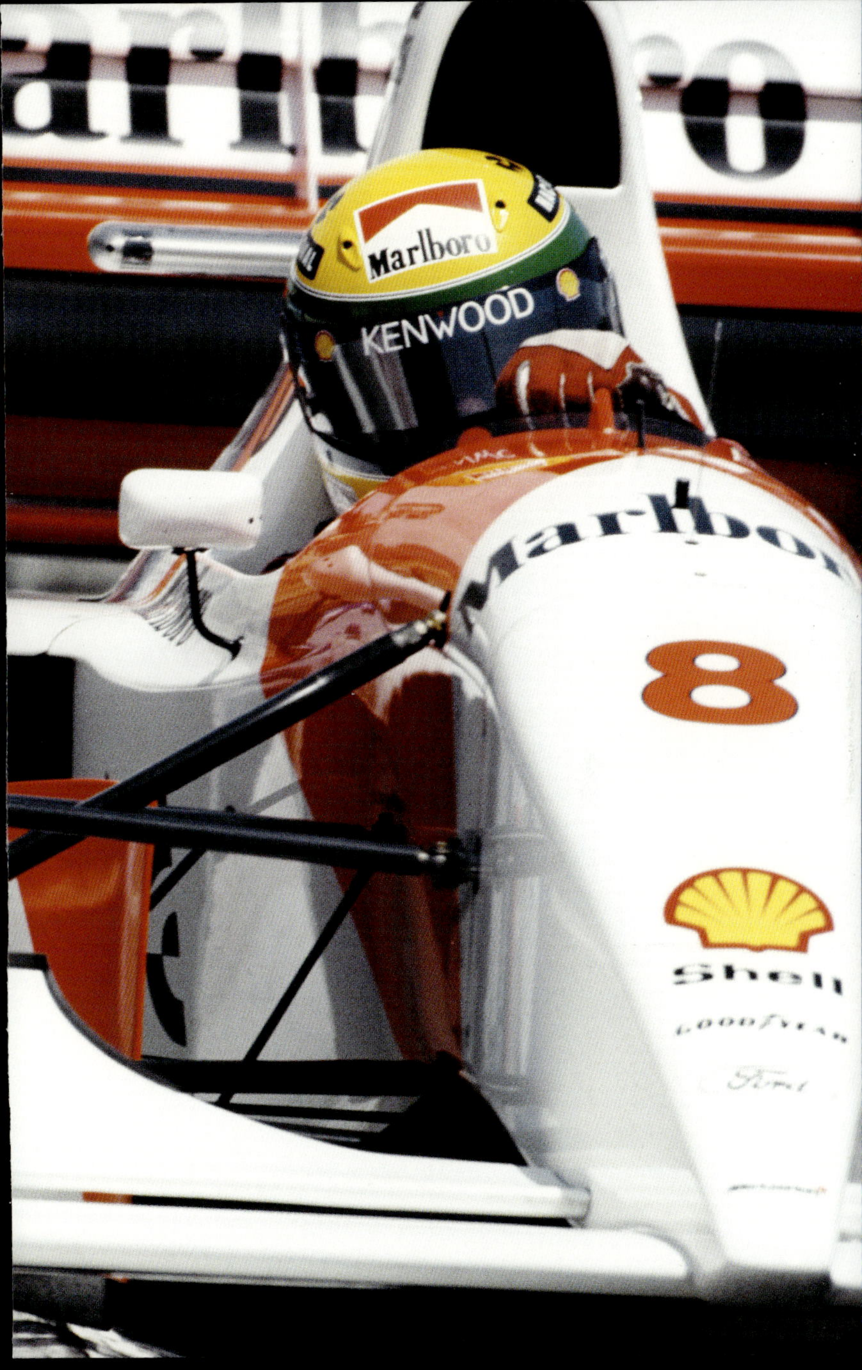
Marlboro
KENWOOD
8
Shell

After Senna had swept to the 1990 world title, which came with McLaren's third successive constructors' championship, Honda insisted on building a V12 engine for 1991. Although Senna and McLaren won the double again, the engine's unexpectedly increased weight and bulk annoyed Senna.

Another new V12 for 1992 could not match the performance of its predecessor and by this point Williams was on the rise again. As McLaren's F1 fortunes waned in 1992, Honda announced it was exiting F1 exactly five years to the day after it had revealed it would be partnering McLaren for the first time.

During the one-year recoupling with Ford in 1993, McLaren built a test mule MP4/8 car with which it secretly tested a Lamborghini V12 engine. The intention was to agree a supply of new engine power for 1994, but, although the unliveried car set times quicker than the Ford-powered race MP4/8, McLaren felt the limited nature of the Lamborghini test programme meant it was better taking a different path for 1994 and its first season post-Senna.

Lamborghini owner Chrysler was said to be "livid" at McLaren's decision to instead sign with Peugeot, according to team biographer William Taylor. The French manufacturer built a new V10 for the MP4/9, but testing only in cool conditions led to struggles at hotter early race events that year – a season in which McLaren added power steering and steering mounted clutch controls for the first time in F1.

Although Peugeot added power to its V10 as 1994 went on – aided by aerodynamic rule changes following Senna's death at Imola that brought engine temperatures down – Dennis sensed another opportunity to boost McLaren through its latest rebuilding phase.

Mercedes had returned to F1 as an engine supplier for Sauber for 1994 but was not satisfied with the state of the team's finances for 1995. Dennis therefore deftly extricated

OPPOSITE: Martin Brundle races the MP4/9 in the 1994 Formula 1 season, which yielded no McLaren wins for the first time since the 1980 campaign.

76 AN ONGOING PROBLEM

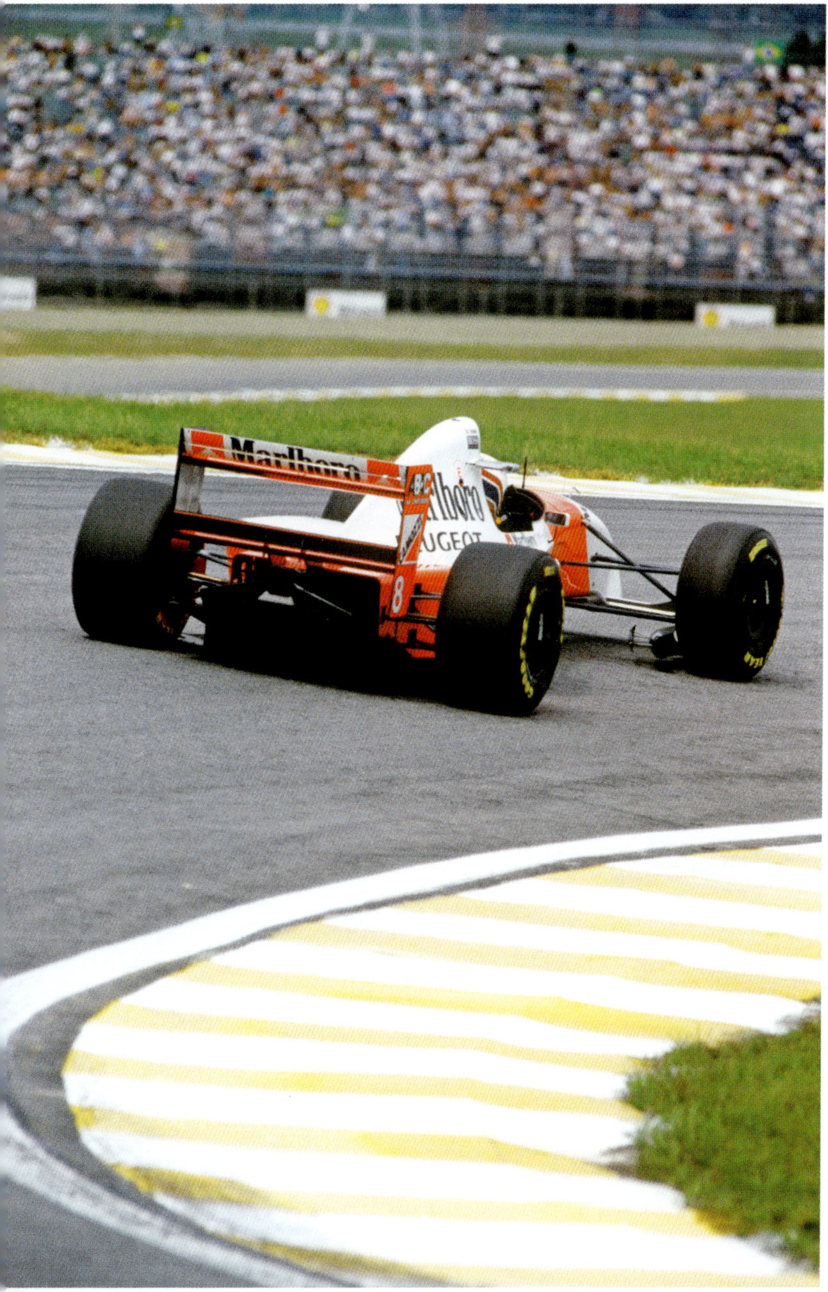
Marlboro

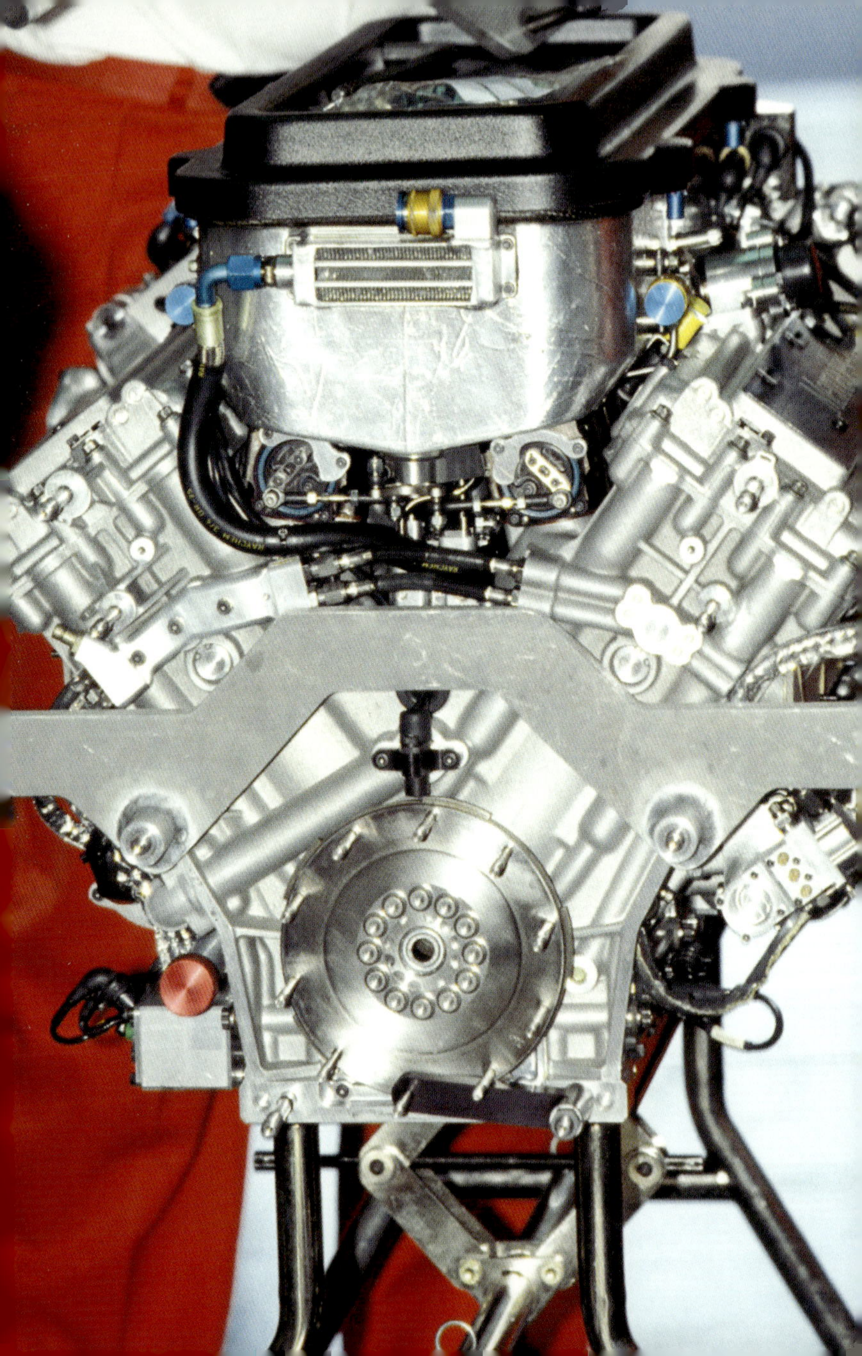

McLaren from its Peugeot deal on good terms and forged its famous partnership with Mercedes.

This came to be class leading – as Mercedes extracted ever more power from its V10 programme. By 1997, the first year after McLaren's long-running partnership with Marlboro had expired and a silver livery with new sponsor West meant the return of the 'Silver Arrows' Mercedes nickname to F1, the manufacturer's engines were producing 740bhp at 16,000rpm.

In the first year of the effectively works Mercedes partnership, the compact V10 meant McLaren could make its F1 chassis smaller – too small for the newly signed Nigel Mansell. McLaren's star driver for the 1995 season lasted just four rounds, only two of which he raced in due to the cockpit size issue, before retiring for good. Fortunately, Mika Häkkinen provided the team with stability on the driving front. This developed into a long-term partnership with new arrival David Coulthard for 1996, after which Häkkinen roared to back-to-back McLaren world title doubles in 1998 and 1999.

The Mercedes deal lasted all through the following decade, in which Ferrari and Michael Schumacher (once a Mercedes junior that the manufacturer and Dennis had hoped to entice to McLaren for 1996 before he headed to Italy) initially dominated.

Kimi Räikkönen's near-misses and Lewis Hamilton's 2008 triumph kept McLaren atop F1 billing through a rule-change to mandatory V8 engines, but after the Brawn GP team secured Mercedes engines for 2009, the company decided it was better off fielding its own squad than just relying on McLaren car prowess.

For another five years, Mercedes nevertheless provided McLaren with customer V8 units. But in 2014 yet another major engine rule change – taking F1 back to turbo power for the first time since the late 1980s but with new hybrid

OPPOSITE: A Mercedes FO 110 V10 engine used by McLaren in the 1995 Formula 1 season – here at that year's French GP. Mercedes would develop the engine to be class leading.

AN ONGOING PROBLEM 79

ABOVE: After its disastrous first season back using Honda engines in 2015, McLaren made a step forward with the RA616H power unit in 2016, but progress soon stalled.

electrification elements this time – vaulted Mercedes to the head of the pecking order, while McLaren languished.

With Martin Whitmarsh now at the helm, McLaren had already long been thinking it needed another works partnership and so turned, once again, to Honda.

The new alliance – announced in 2013 for a 2015 commencement – hoped to recapture the old magic. As Hamilton was now racking up titles for Mercedes, former Honda and Brawn GP star Jenson Button was to be partnered with another established champion (and controversial former McLaren star), Fernando Alonso.

But Honda's first V6 turbos were beset by problems and McLaren's expected uplift failed to materialize. After three frustrating years, McLaren opted to become a customer engine squad once again – this time doing a deal with Renault that evoked memories of Alonso's two titles in 2005 and 2006 for the French OEM giant.

This too, did not last, and in 2021 McLaren returned to buying in Mercedes engines. This arrangement is set to last until at least 2030 in F1 and well into the championship's upcoming new engine rules era from 2026 – in which hybrid systems will be simplified.

After Daniel Ricciardo's 2021 Italian GP win and McLaren's 2024 successes with Lando Norris and Oscar Piastri, its win total with Mercedes power sits at 81 GPs. Next up is Honda on 43.

BELOW: McLaren used Renault engines for the first time in Formula 1 in between 2018 and 2020, with the partnership yielding three podiums but no victories

WRITING
LEGENDS

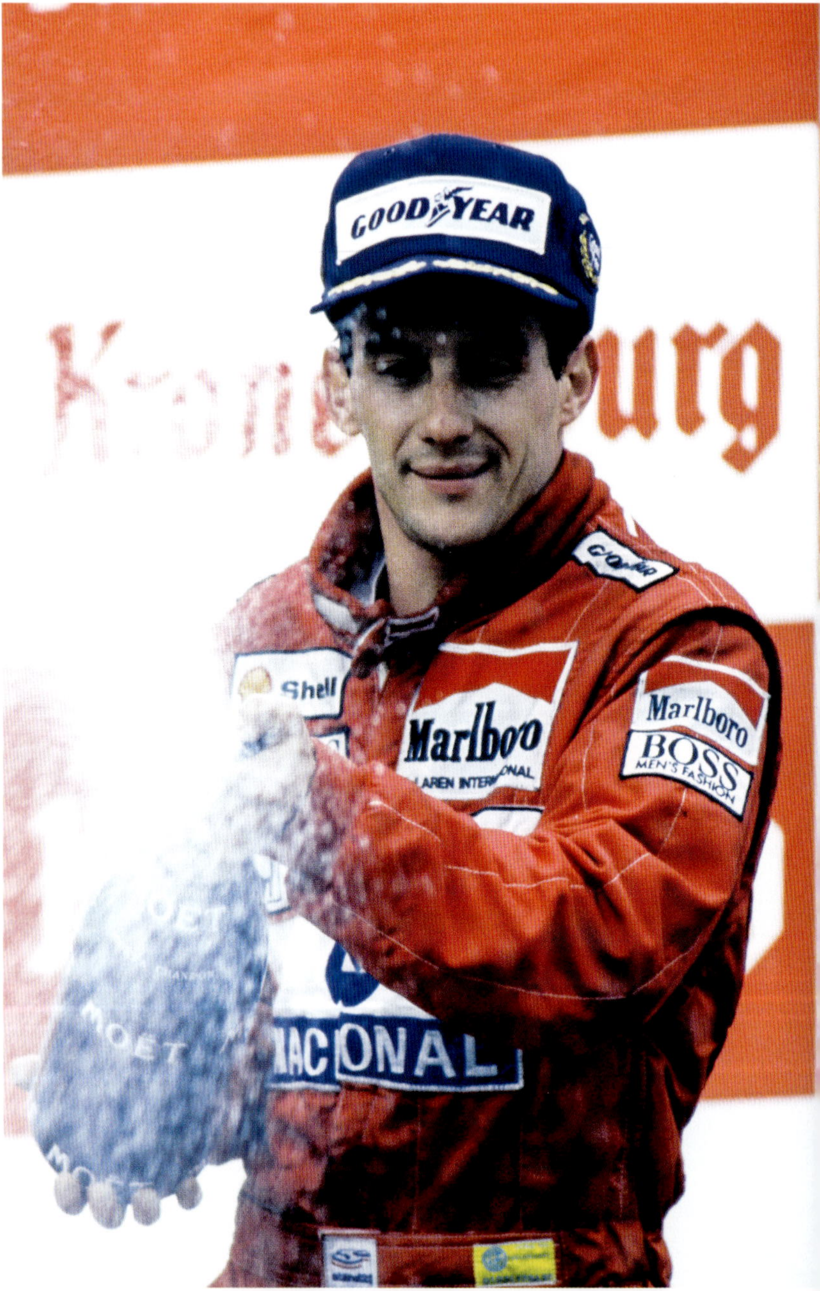
GOODYEAR
Shell
Marlboro
Marlboro
BOSS
MEN'S FASHION

THE HEROES:
SENNA, HÄKKINEN, HAMILTON

Since the formation of the Formula 1 world championship in 1950, 34 racers have clinched the drivers' title. Seven of them with McLaren.

But of this distinct crop of champions, a trio stands clear. Either for how McLaren became central to their own legend, for securing special status within the team, or for how McLaren helped them commence a unique story of F1 achievement. These drivers are Ayrton Senna, Mika Häkkinen and Lewis Hamilton.

In 1988, Senna joined McLaren from Lotus, where he had taken a pair of victories each year since making his 1984 debut with Toleman. His reputation was of an ace young driver going places fast – and keen to arrive even quicker.

OPPOSITE: Ayrton Senna celebrates winning the 1988 San Marino GP.

WRITING LEGENDS

ABOVE: Ayrton Senna in the 1988 Japanese GP – a race where he would start on pole, stall at the start and yet race back to win and seal his first Formula 1 world title.

Autosport magazine said, "he made Lotus – virtually from the day he arrived – into his team, but this is out of the question at McLaren", ahead of his first appearance for Ron Dennis's squad.

That year was also the debut of the McLaren MP4/4. In the hands of Senna and teammate Prost, the Honda-powered turbo car would win 15 from 16 races, a win success rate of 93.8 per cent that was only beaten in 2023 by the Red Bull RB19's 95.5 per cent. Had it not been for a clash while overtaking a backmarker at the Italian GP that put Senna out from the lead late on, McLaren would have taken an historic clean sweep.

Senna had been obsessed with winning the 1988 title. As he prevailed with a great drive in the Japanese GP to seal his first F1 career crown, his fight with Prost had been intense but respectful.

The following year, their relationship descended into acrimony. With both challenging once again in the MP4/4's successor, they collided in the closing stages of that year's Japanese GP. As Prost climbed from his MP4/5, Senna got going again after being pushed by track safety marshals and went on to win – but was controversially disqualified soon afterwards. This move, which Senna felt had been politically engineered with officials and was subsequently upheld in court after McLaren appealed, meant Prost regained his crown.

But Prost had already had enough. He moved to Ferrari for 1990, leaving Senna to lead McLaren alongside his friend Gerhard Berger. Once again, Senna and Prost were the title protagonists and again the outcome of their battle was decided at the Suzuka circuit.

ABOVE: Ayrton Senna with Gerhard Berger at the 1991 Brazilian GP. The pair were good friends, following Senna's tempestuous relationship with previous McLaren teammate, Alan Prost.

Although there was a race in Australia remaining, Senna's points lead meant he held a commanding position, but he was left furious by the Suzuka event organizers deciding to keep the pole position grid spot away from the racing line and the extra grip it gave tyres at race starts.

As Prost nipped ahead on that line at the race's start, Senna kept his throttle pinned at the track's first corner – triggering a crash that put both drivers out but secured his 1990 crown. Then McLaren team principal Dennis later told Senna: "I'm disappointed in you".

The following 1991 campaign was arguably Senna's high point with McLaren. He dominated the season with seven wins – including his first triumph at his home race in Brazil, where he won despite suffering severe shoulder cramp battling on with a gearbox problem.

In 1992, the Williams team led by Nigel Mansell knocked McLaren off its perch as F1's dominant team. This was largely thanks to its FW14B car's active suspension system that McLaren lacked, plus Honda's engine that year being delayed and fuel-demanding. Senna nevertheless won three races to Mansell's nine. The following year he took five more victories and finished as runner-up to Prost, who was now leading Williams, which continued to dominate.

The 1993 campaign took in another legendary Senna win – his triumph at Donington in that year's European GP, where he famously charged from fourth to first on the race's opening lap. But McLaren and Senna were headed for a split. Negotiations over money lasted long into the year and the sophisticated MP4/8 nevertheless proved unreliable.

He eventually left to join Williams himself for 1994, and died tragically in May of that year. But Senna's ability to inspire left a memory felt at McLaren to this day.

BELOW: The 1993 European GP at Donington is considered one of Ayrton Senna's finest Formula 1 wins. He even lost a place at the start before charging into the lead.

RIGHT: Ayrton Senna joining Williams for 1994 would later impact Ron Dennis's consideration of his greatest McLaren drivers – Dennis prized loyalty.

OPPOSITE: Mika Häkkinen made a splash when he finally appeared as a race driver for McLaren, qualifying third for the 1993 Portuguese GP ahead of Ayrton Senna.

Dennis would one day pick Häkkinen as the greatest driver he had ever employed – in part because, unlike Senna, he had stuck things out with McLaren even after losing his place atop the F1 pecking order. That was to come against Michael Schumacher and Ferrari in 2000, but Häkkinen's relationship with Dennis went back over a decade earlier, when the Finn applied to join the Marlboro World Championship Team for 1988, which backed young drivers. Dennis was on the judging panel, given his long history with the cigarette company and its sponsor dealmakers.

Häkkinen entered F1 in 1991, where he made his debut with Lotus. He showed promise in a team that was a shadow of its former self – scrapping for positions well down grid. After a second learning year at Lotus, Häkkinen was among the many that hoped to move to the then dominant Williams team.

Ultimately his efforts were thwarted in a contractual wrangling with Lotus, which later led to a deal with Dennis to become McLaren's test driver for 1993, after Senna decided to carry on racing for the team after all.

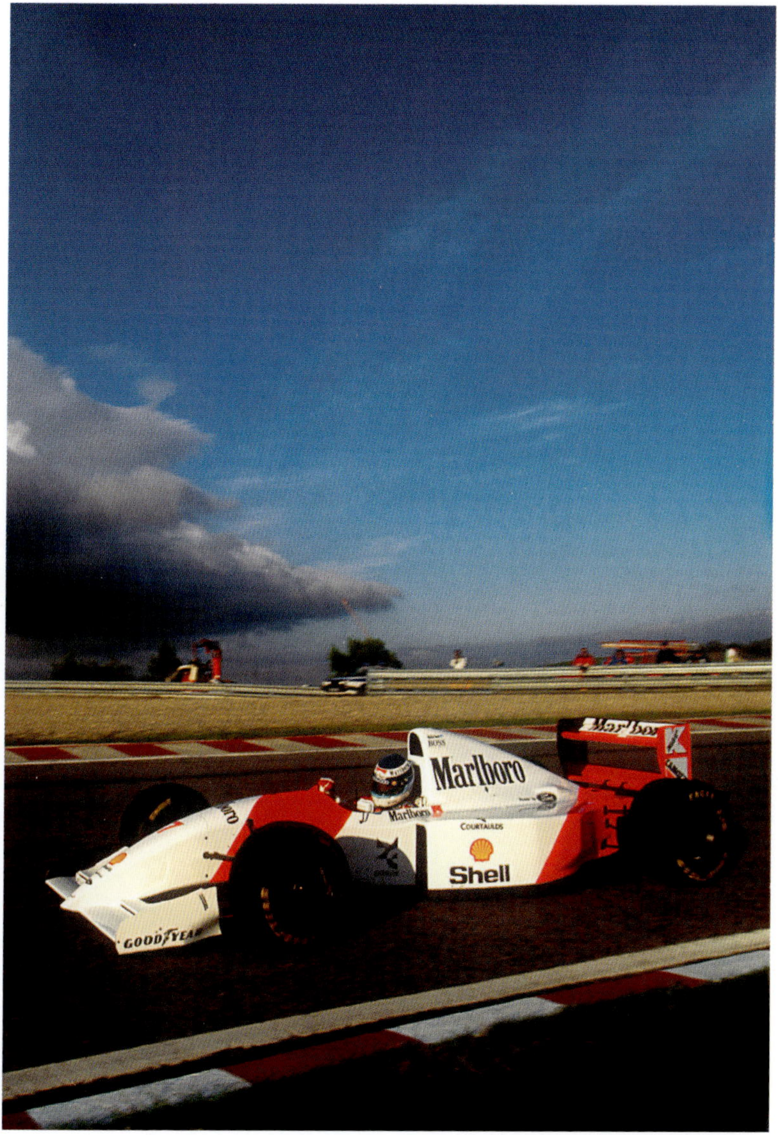
Marlboro
Shell
COURTAULDS
GOODYEAR
BOSS

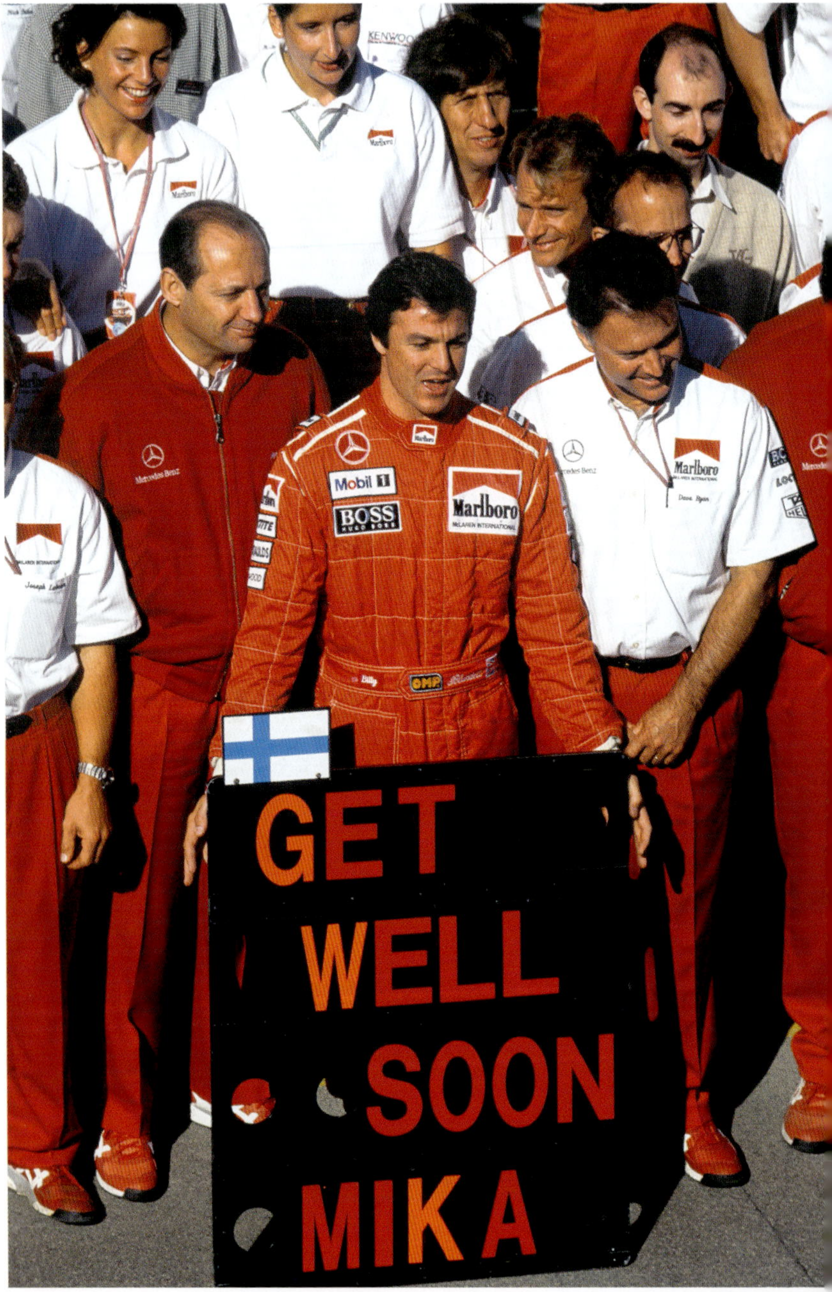
GET
WELL
SOON
MIKA
Marlboro
Mobil 1
BOSS

When Michael Andretti left his position as Senna's teammate with three races remaining, Häkkinen got his big chance – and immediately seized it at the 1993 Portuguese GP. He out-qualified Senna – enraging the famous Brazilian. Häkkinen, however, refused to revel in his accomplishments and quietly set about his task. This became taking over as McLaren's lead driver for 1994.

That year, he scored six podiums in addition to the one he had taken the previous season, but McLaren's MP4/9 again lacked class-leading pedigree, plus reliability in the team's one year using Peugeot power.

The 1995 season was a similar story. McLaren showed promise, now in the first year of its Mercedes engine supply deal, but was frustrated with reliability problems. It all ended in dramatic circumstances for Häkkinen. In Friday qualifying for the season-concluding Australian GP, the Finn crashed hard after suffering a sudden puncture. His impact with the barriers left him with a fractured skull, with an emergency tracheotomy performed to save his life trackside.

Dennis visited him in hospital, shocked that a driver had nearly died in a car for which he had responsibility for the first time in his career. A long, painful recovery followed – including subsequent surgery – but Häkkinen recovered in time to test McLaren's 1996 car just 12 weeks after his Adelaide crash. He was soon lapping quicker than Schumacher – a junior formula rival of Mika's – who had been practising with his new Ferrari team at the same Paul Ricard track.

That season was the first of five tension-filled championships in which Häkkinen led McLaren alongside David Coulthard. Already a race winner, which Häkkinen envied, Coulthard would come to feel Dennis was subconsciously prioritizing his teammate. Dennis later confirmed this was the case because of the lingering trauma of Häkkinen's crash.

OPPOSITE: Mark Blundell with McLaren team staff at the 1995 Australian GP, wishing Mika Häkkinen a swift recovery after his shocking crash in qualifying.

WRITING LEGENDS

After a solid but unspectacular 1996 season on his return from injury, Häkkinen finally became an F1 race winner at the end of the 1997 campaign, when eventual champion Jacques Villeneuve gifted him victory in the season-concluding Jerez race. Although contrived, it relieved the pressure he had been facing at having started nearly 100 races without winning. Now in 1998 and 1999, Häkkinen's golden era arrived.

Although he was still suffering with regular headaches because of his 1995 injuries, he emerged triumphant in a famous 1998 title fight with Schumacher. This was in the first McLaren – the MP4-13 – designed by the highly rated engineer, Adrian Newey. Häkkinen doubled up in 1999, even as Newey's second McLaren creation proved fast but fragile.

In 2000, Schumacher and Ferrari finally bested McLaren. But that season included Häkkinen's tenacious pass on his great rival either side of a slower backmarker at the Belgian GP. This moment was another reason why Dennis, who had been vindicated in signing and then sticking by the 'Flying Finn' for so long before his titles arrived, rates Häkkinen so highly in his consideration of the best McLaren drivers.

The other is Hamilton, whose F1 legend started with McLaren. He followed Häkkinen as the team's next world champion – following the near-misses of Kimi Räikkönen, another fast, taciturn Finn – in 2003 and 2005. In winning the 2008 world title, Hamilton ended an eight-year championship drought, as McLaren had likewise endured seven between Senna's final title triumph and Häkkinen's first.

Hamilton had also been introduced to Dennis long before he arrived in F1. The Briton attended the 1995 *Autosport* Awards – an annual prize-giving ceremony hosted by the magazine – as a ten-year-old go-kart racer accepting a trophy. There, he "went up to Ron and said I wanted to race his car and be world champion", as Hamilton would recall in 2007. Dennis

OPPOSITE: Mika Häkkinen celebrates winning the 1999 Japanese GP at Suzuka, which sealed his second successive Formula 1 world championship for McLaren.

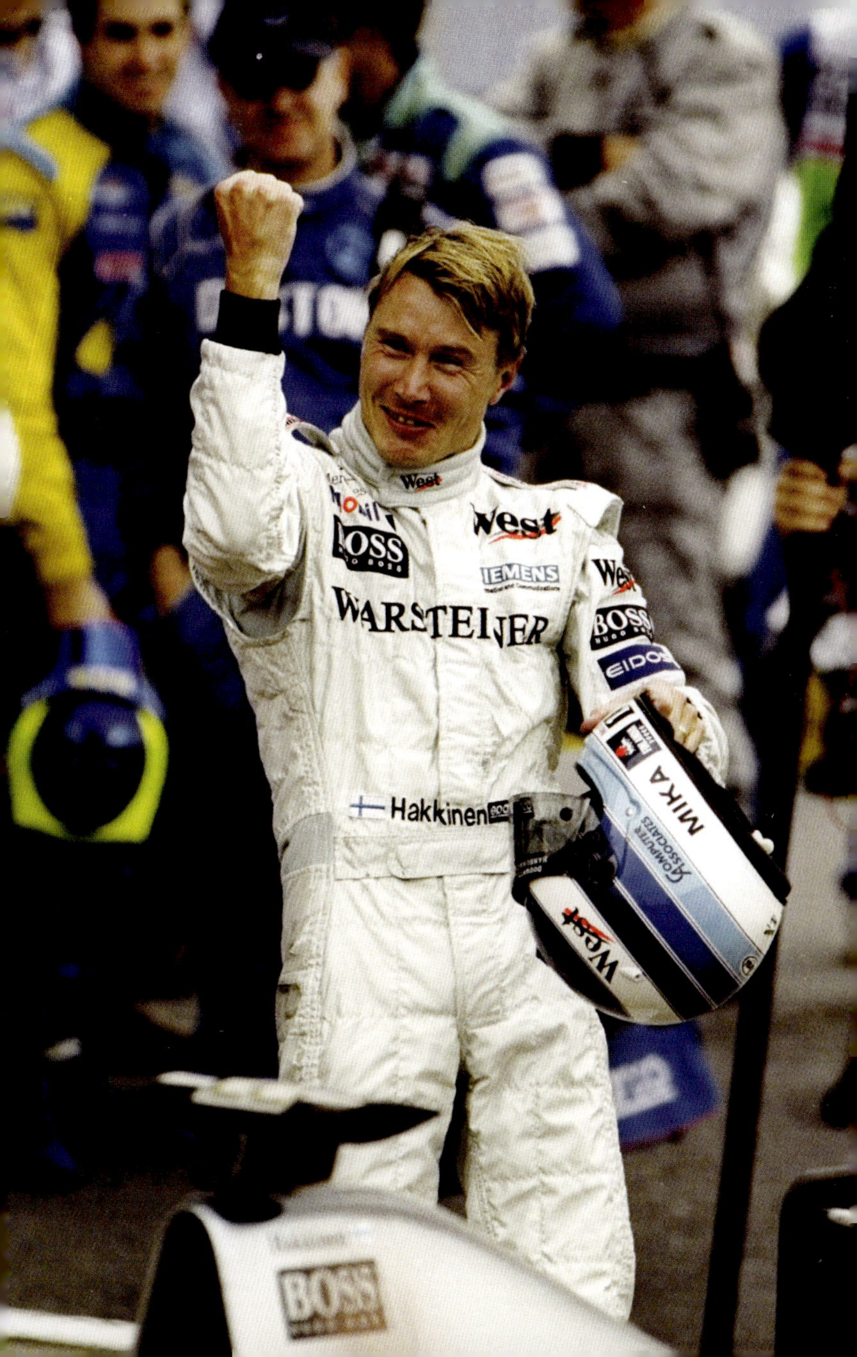
West
BOSS
West
BOSS
EIDOS
Hakkinen
MIKA
West
BOSS

ABOVE: Lewis Hamilton and Ron Dennis at the Kimbolton Kart Circuit in England. Dennis would promote Hamilton to race in Formula 1 for McLaren in 2007.

initially told Hamilton to get back in touch nine years later, but in 1998 he signed him to McLaren's young driver development programme.

Hamilton duly climbed the ranks. By late 2006, he was giving Dennis and his key lieutenant, Martin Whitmarsh, little choice in fast-tracking his rise to F1. And so, ahead of the 2007 season in which Räikkönen replaced the exiting Schumacher at Ferrari, Dennis made Hamilton McLaren's first rookie F1 racer since 1995's Pacific GP (where Häkkinen was replaced for one race by the Dane Jan Magnussen following an appendectomy). This broke a long tradition of not selecting rookies that had developed during the team's various runs at the pinnacle of the F1 pecking order.

Hamilton made an instant impression – finishing on the podium at the season opener in Australia and in doing so overtaking his teammate, the reigning world champion, Fernando Alonso, who had just arrived from Renault.

Hamilton had been well prepared by McLaren through his time as a junior, when he was entrusted with testing new F1 cars in minor tests, as one of the team's then-race engineers, Dave Robson, recalled in 2021 after Hamilton had become the first F1 driver to score 100 grand prix poles.

"There was that special quality you can't really define," said Robson. "That was obvious right from when he was just a kid and they took him testing at Elvington [airfield] – going up and down the runway – and he was bored stiff after ten minutes.

"Whereas most kids, when you took them to Elvington, they were just chuffed to bits being in an F1 car – even though they were just going up and down the runway. Lewis was different right from the beginning."

Hamilton was soon winning for McLaren – taking his first triumph in the 2007 Canadian GP. But a schism was developing with Alonso, who was later involved in revealing the Spygate scandal that would come to cost McLaren dearly.

Dennis was resolute in backing Hamilton that year, with Alonso soon deciding he would rather leave for 2008 (he rejoined Renault). The pair nevertheless fought hard for the 2007 world title, with Hamilton losing out in large part due to McLaren's strategy of running wet tyres during that year's Chinese GP. He eventually slipped off the road due to his rubber wearing and retired. After gearbox software trouble for Hamilton at the start of the season finale in Brazil, Räikkönen pipped the McLaren pair to the championship crown.

The following campaign was another classic, in which Hamilton this time emerged with the title despite another

ABOVE: Lewis Hamilton wins the 2008 British GP for McLaren – considered one of his best F1 victories.

OPPOSITE: Forced retirements in 2012, such as here in Singapore, contributed to Hamilton's decision to leave McLaren and join Mercedes.

OVERLEAF: Hamilton scored his final McLaren F1 victory in the 2012 United States GP in Texas – featuring novelty podium hats.

dramatic final race in Brazil. Dennis would later insist Hamilton's result in the wet-dry-wet thriller was down to McLaren's disciplined professionalism and not luck.

Disappointing car designs, unreliability and the rise of the Red Bull team would mean Hamilton and the squad, now helmed by Dennis's anointed successor, Whitmarsh, would not win another title post-2008.

But the driver Dennis prized for his speed and uncompromising attitude still has a fondness for his first team, even after leaving it in 2013 to join the Mercedes squad. There he secured the majority of his seven titles and record F1 race victory haul.

"That's my old, original family," Hamilton said after finishing third behind Oscar Piastri and Lando Norris in the 2024 Hungarian GP, where McLaren finished an F1 race with its cars 1-2 in the order for the only the second time in 14 years.

"I'm really happy to see you, all the boys, the whole team, back up front."

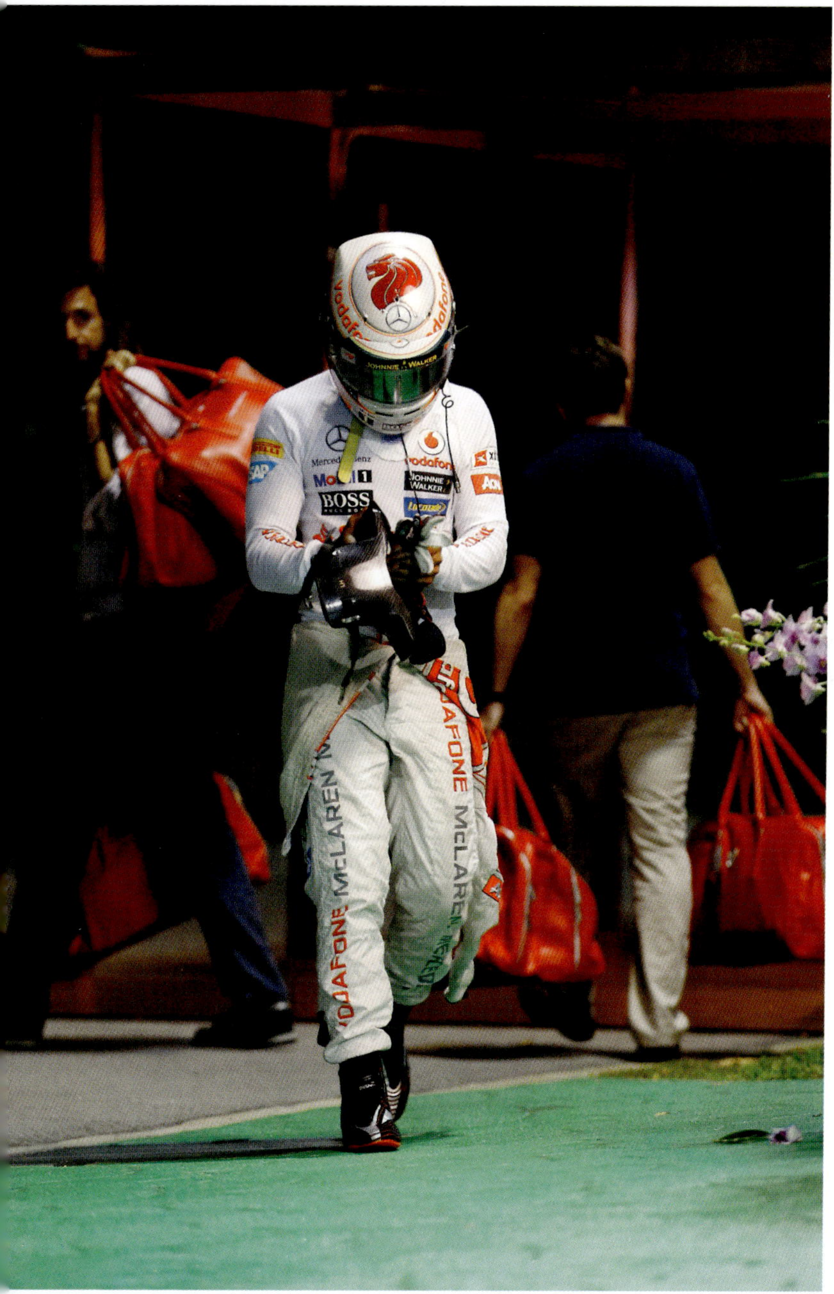
vodafone
JOHNNIE WALKER
vodafone
BOSS
McLAREN
VODAFONE

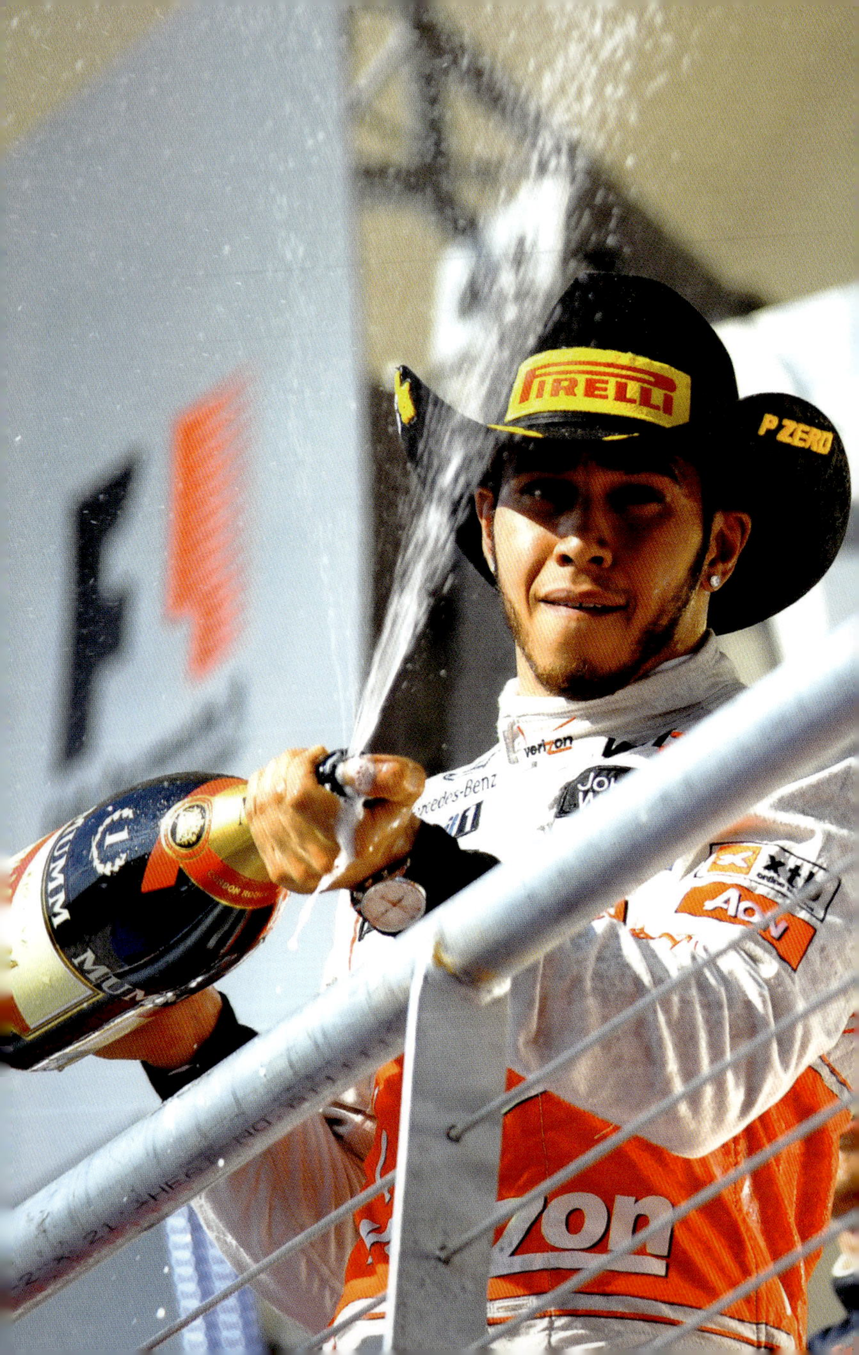
PIRELLI
P ZERO
MUMM
Aon

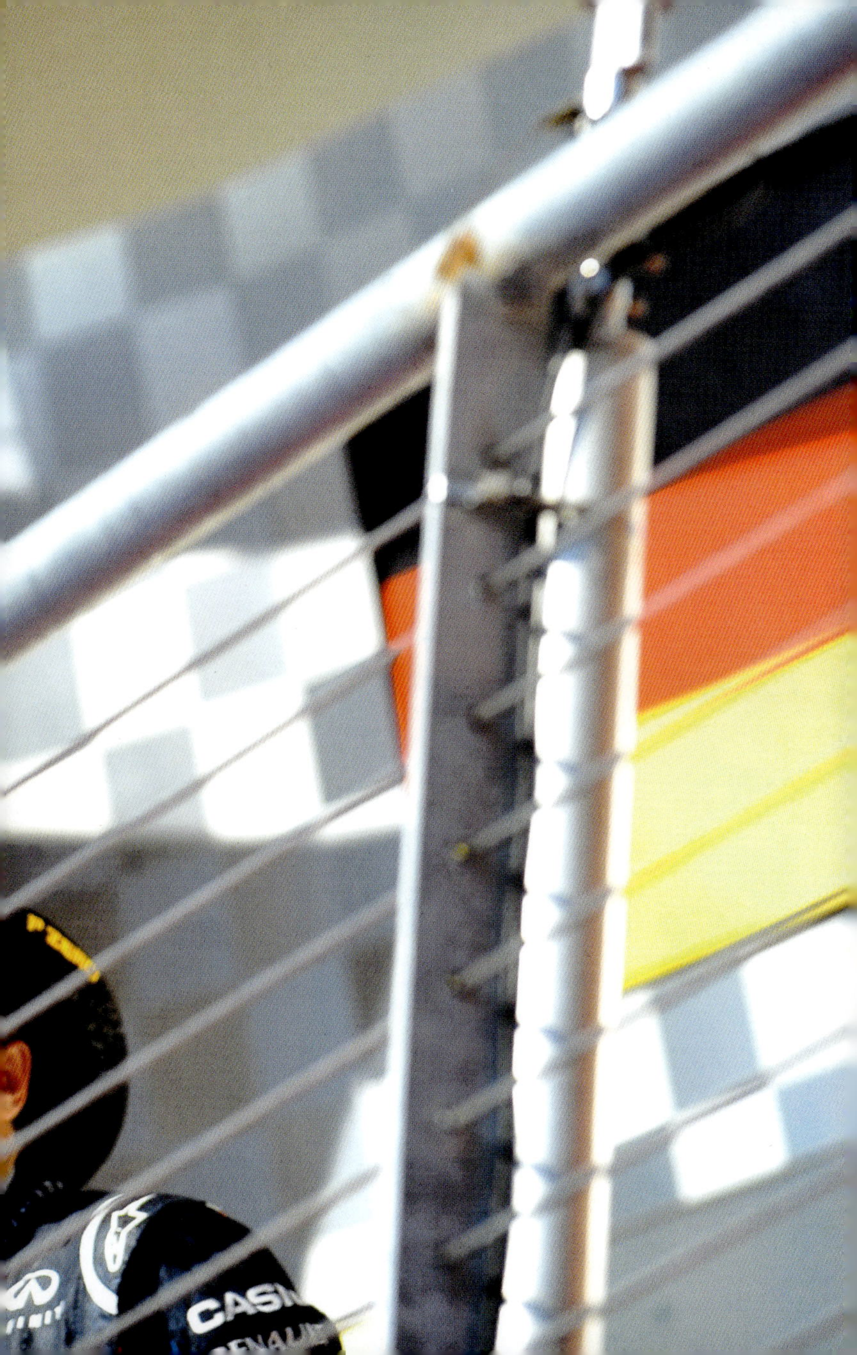

CLASH OF THE
TITANS

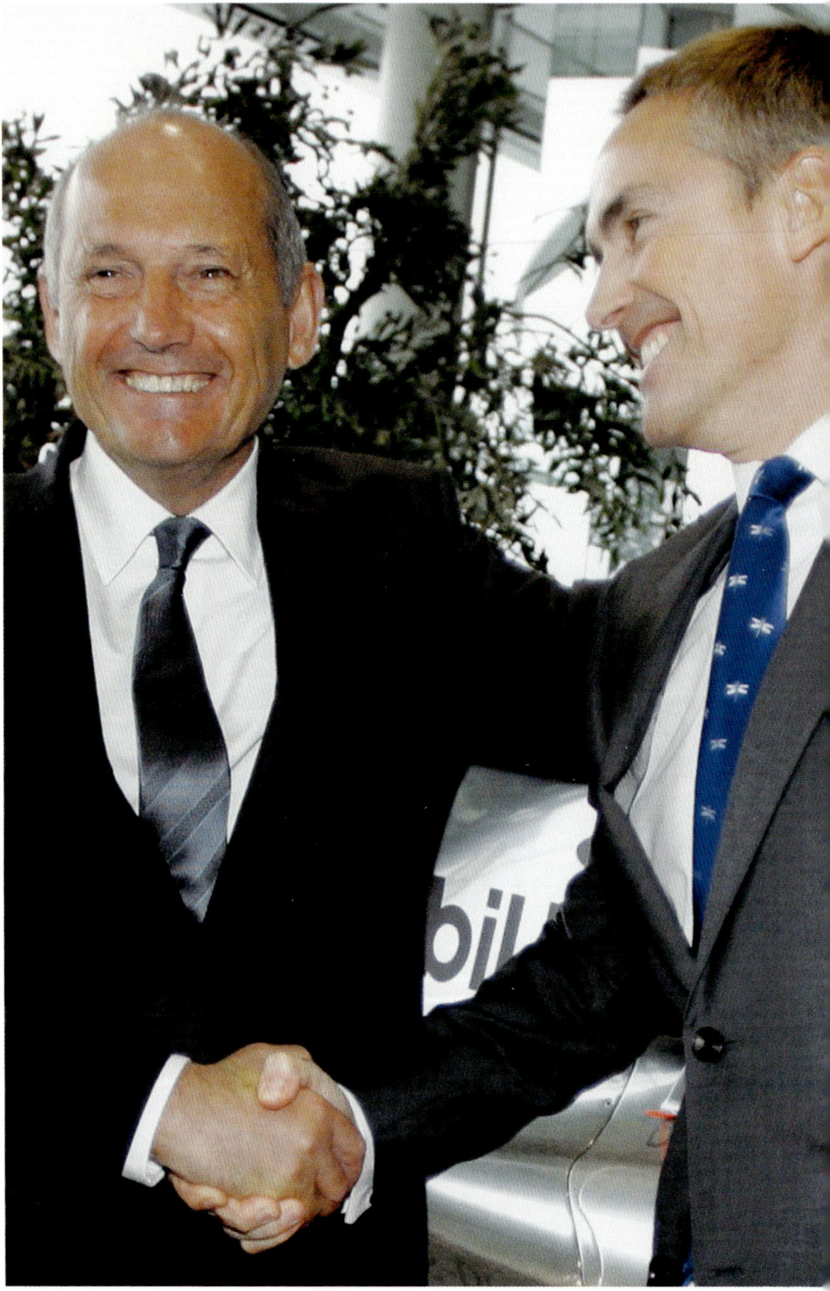

THE SUCCESSOR: MARTIN WHITMARSH

McLaren was riding the crest of a wave as the late 2000s unfurled. Ron Dennis's long-held dream of the company becoming a major automotive power was becoming reality and its Formula 1 team was still winning races and competing for championships. In 2007, its promising junior driver Lewis Hamilton was promoted to grand prix racing and made an instant impact. But sparks that would become flames of disaster were already igniting.

Before promoting Hamilton, McLaren had already moved to secure its long-term F1 driver future by signing Fernando Alonso from Renault back in 2005. This was just after the Spaniard had won his first of two world titles for the French marque, with the other coming in 2006, when Hamilton won an eye-catching GP2 title on the F1 support bill.

OPPOSITE: Whitmarsh was announced as McLaren team boss in early 2009.

ABOVE: McLaren's MP4-24 car was a disappointment in 2009, but the team improved its performance enough for Lewis Hamilton to scoop victories in Hungary and Singapore.

Having arrived expecting to be McLaren's star driver, tensions with the politically agitating Alonso soon arose. These came to a head during the 2007 season's Hungarian Grand Prix. There, Alonso blocked Hamilton in the pitlane during qualifying and was later penalized. But the fallout from the incident revealed a much bigger problem.

Dennis was to then discover that Alonso – plus team test driver Pedro de la Rosa – had been discussing confidential data about the Ferrari team's car that year. In what came to be known as the Spygate scandal, it soon emerged that a Ferrari employee had shared a dossier of design details with McLaren chief designer Mike Coughlan and the case was soon in court when motorsport's governing body, the FIA, had been alerted to the story.

McLaren was eventually handed a $100 million fine – at the time declared a record in sport. While Dennis railed against the punishment, FIA president Max Mosley would claim before his death in 2021 that only £5 million of the fine had been for "what you did" and the rest due to a combustible relationship with Dennis.

The McLaren team was made to forfeit its 2007 constructors' championship points – although the drivers, who were given a degree of immunity from the FIA for co-operating with its investigation, were allowed to keep their personal points and wins. Come the season's end, former McLaren racer Kimi Räikkönen beat Hamilton and Alonso by one point to win the drivers' title for Ferrari.

Alonso departed, but far worse was the reputational damage done to McLaren's brand. It soon became clear that the 2008 campaign would be Dennis's last as McLaren's F1 team boss. But he denied the Spygate affair was resulting in his exit – claiming at the time "my personal future has never been in question" and indicating that it simply crystalized his plans for succession once he had helped "steer the company through this very difficult period".

He would hand power in the McLaren F1 team to a man who had been central to its ongoing success since the late 1980s and had long been a key Dennis lieutenant. This was Martin Whitmarsh.

Whitmarsh had joined McLaren in 1989 as operations director. From an engineering background, he had previously worked for defence systems manufacturer British Aerospace. It was there that he learned the system that he would make famous at McLaren. This was a 'matrix' management approach that meant a flat structure with multiple reporting lines instead of a hierarchy arrangement. It was eventually included in McLaren's F1 car design department and later led to the departure of Adrian Newey, who detested the system, in the mid-2000s.

Whitmarsh would climb McLaren's ranks and is credited with making Dennis's wider vision for expanding the organization a reality. In 1997, he was made the team's managing director and in 2004 was appointed chief operating officer of the McLaren Group. In the intervening time, he had played a key role in planning and developing Hamilton's junior career. By 2008, Whitmarsh and Dennis were already sharing many of the jobs an F1 team principal conducts, to ease the eventual handover.

That came in January 2009, when Whitmarsh said he was "massively privileged" to be appointed McLaren F1 team boss – with the target of defending the title Hamilton had won in dramatic circumstances at the 2008 Brazilian GP, plus scoring McLaren's first constructors' championship since 1998. Dennis, meanwhile, would concentrate on launching McLaren's automotive arm as Group chairman and CEO.

Whitmarsh's promotion to team boss coincided with a new era of F1 car design. The regulations for 2009 required the teams to drop many of the aerodynamic parts that had previously made the old cars so fast and complex, as the FIA was concerned about mounting speeds.

McLaren had been involved in drafting the new rules due to its membership of the FIA's Overtaking Working Group, which at the time looked at car design rules to try and improve F1's racing entertainment spectacle. McLaren believed its 2009 design had met the reduction in downforce targets exactly and so would be in a strong position for the campaign.

But, before it discovered this was not the case, Whitmarsh made what has come to be viewed as a major mistake.

This was to allow the McLaren's exclusivity arrangement to run Mercedes' F1 engines – an agreement that had been

OPPOSITE: Future McLaren driver Jenson Button on his way to winning the 2009 Australian GP – the year Whitmarsh gave up McLaren's exclusivity deal to use Mercedes engines.

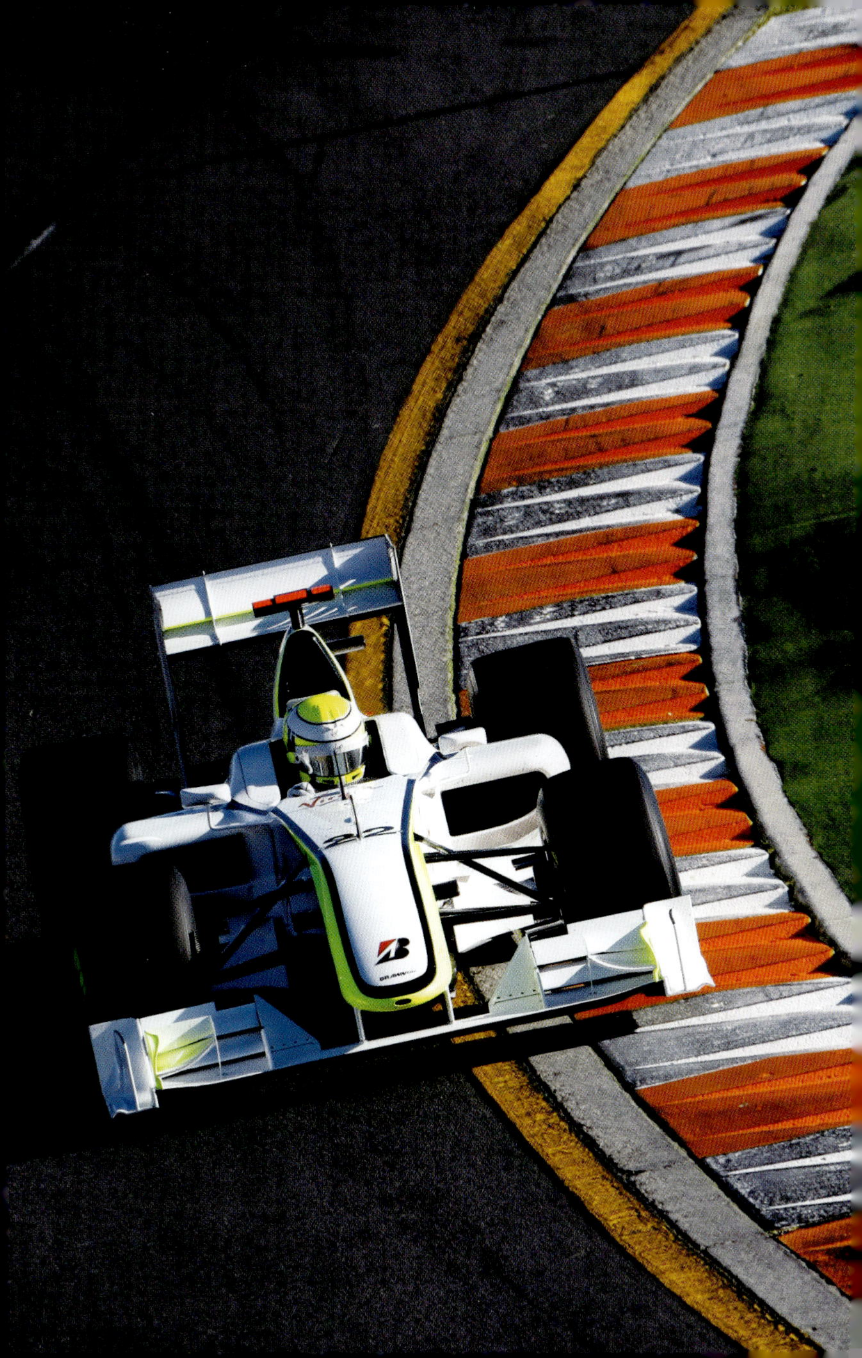

110 CLASH OF THE TITANS

unbroken since 1995 and continued to be viewed as class-leading even after F1's rules on power units meant they were all V8s from 2006 – to be diluted.

It was a special and famous case. The former Honda works team had been on the cusp of closing when its management – led by team principal and famed F1 engineer Ross Brawn – had stepped in to buy the team and try to save it through 2009. Progress was made, but what was now Brawn GP still needed an engine or it would fold before ever racing.

Here, Whitmarsh was eyeing the chairmanship of the Formula One Teams' Association organization, which opposed the FIA's plans to change F1's rules amid wider renegotiations of its commercial structures. He agreed to help Brawn, and would indeed later go on to helm the Teams' Association.

McLaren insiders now view Whitmarsh's choice as him wanting to be seen as a statesman-like figure in the wider F1 world by helping to save another squad. And while this did maintain the championship's overall sporting health, at the same time many of his staff were suddenly wary about what this might mean for the team's future now Mercedes had had its head turned by a second engine customer.

The Brawn GP car would prove to have 2009's best aerodynamic platform with its infamous double diffuser development. The Williams and Toyota teams also had this device, but its ability to claw back the downforce lost in the rule changes had been dismissed by the teams including McLaren that formed the OWG.

Brawn won both championships that year, while McLaren somewhat saved its season with what Hamilton called "the worst car that I had driven, apart from the engine was good", as he won two races following urgent redesign work. The bigger problem for McLaren was what this all meant for Mercedes from 2010.

OPPOSITE: Lewis Hamilton celebrates winning the 2009 Hungarian GP. After his 2008 world title success, he was unimpressed by McLaren's subsequent chassis design under F1's new rules.

ABOVE: McLaren signed Jenson Button for the 2010 Formula 1 season after he had won the 2009 world title for Brawn GP, creating a strong line-up with Lewis Hamilton.

OPPOSITE: In another disappointing season, despite the novel design of McLaren's MP4-26, Hamilton scored an impressive win in the 2011 Chinese GP ahead of Red Bull's Sebastian Vettel.

The German automotive giant, which had given McLaren "crucial" backing, according to *Autosport* in 2007 during Spygate, decided it would now rather fund its own team and it purchased the Brawn squad. Mercedes then gradually exited the 40 per cent shareholding it had in the McLaren F1 team, with its ownership stake passing to the McLaren Group.

McLaren and Hamilton – plus 2009 world champion Jenson Button, who had been lured from Mercedes in something of a coup for McLaren late in the year that he won his title – challenged for the 2010 and 2012 world titles. But McLaren's star had really started to wane.

The rising Red Bull team was now hoovering up championships ahead of many of F1's long-established squads, while the matrix management style came to be viewed as responsible for successive McLaren cars having disappointing designs. By late 2012, when McLaren's MP4-27 was quick but very fragile, Hamilton decided he had had enough of seeing Red Bull's Sebastian Vettel race to four world titles when he

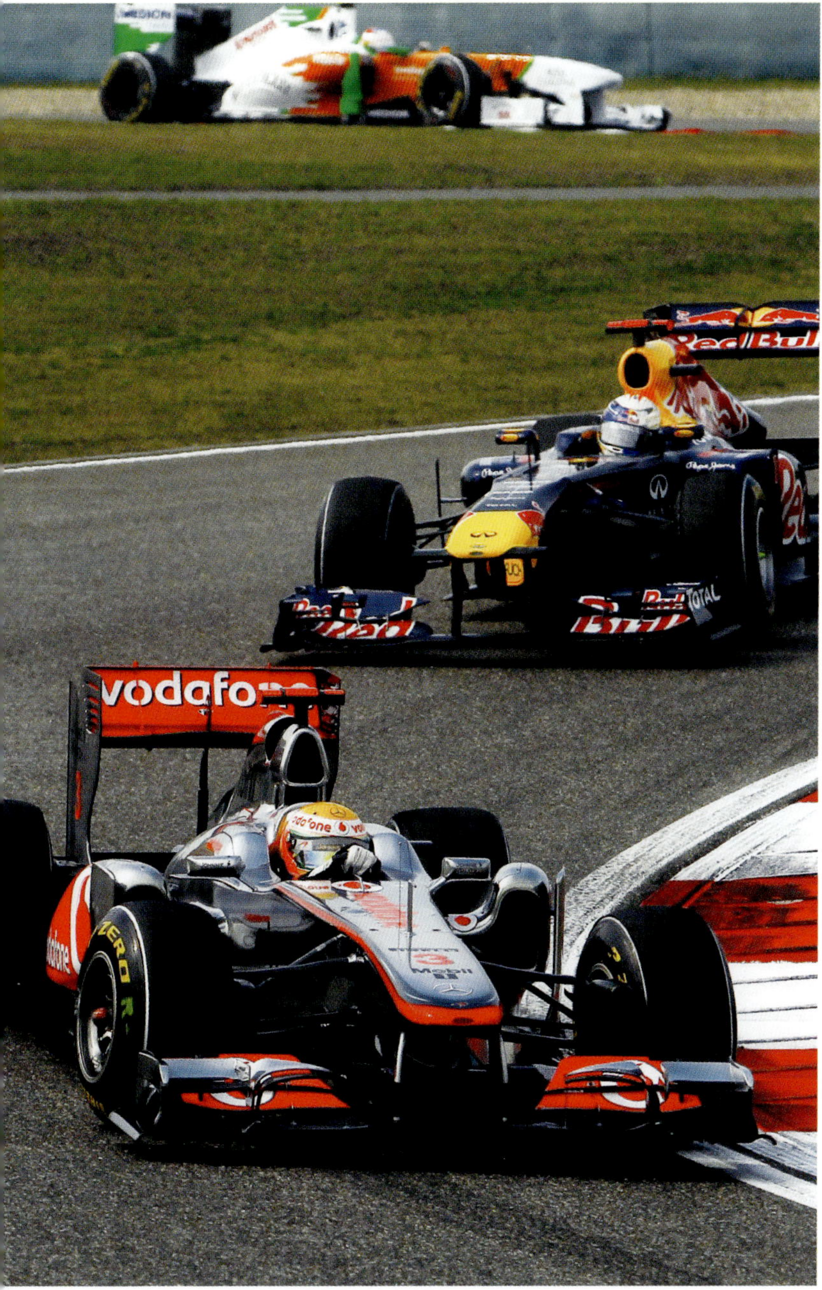
TOTAL

ABOVE: Jenson Button's victory in the wild 2012 Brazilian GP was to be McLaren's last in Formula 1 for almost nine years, amid the rise of the Red Bull and Mercedes teams.

still only had the 2008 crown. He was convinced to leave the team that had raised him in F1.

After Hamilton decided to join Mercedes for 2013, Button won McLaren the 2012 season-ending Brazilian GP. Its road cars were gaining considerable respect in the automotive world, but now Bruce's team was about to enter its longest-ever silverware drought.

Whitmarsh signed young driver Sergio Pérez to partner Button for 2013 – a year in which McLaren made a bold call that backfired in abandoning 2012's relatively successful design and pursuing a new concept that failed with just one year before the next major rule change arrived in 2014. This shift introduced V6 turbo engines back into F1, although with new hybrid elements. With these engines, Hamilton and Mercedes would go on to dominate the championship. McLaren, as a customer team, could not compete.

But by this point Whitmarsh's time helming its F1 squad was over. He and Dennis had fallen out spectacularly, with Dennis even trying to remove his former protégé from his post on several occasions in the two years running up to 2014. Ironically, these attempts failed because of his similarly strained relations with fellow board members. Mansour Ojjeh was said to have been most upset by Dennis's treatment of Whitmarsh.

After finally acting in January 2014, Dennis said the board had "mandated me to write an exciting new chapter in the story of McLaren, beginning by improving our on-track and off-track performance".

BELOW: Sergio Pérez (right) was signed to replace Lewis Hamilton alongside Jenson Button for the 2013 Formula 1 season. But he lasted only one season in McLaren's line-up.

ABOVE: Whitmarsh on the McLaren team's pitwall stand at the 2013 Brazilian GP, which was to be his last running the Formula 1 team.

Before he left, Whitmarsh had approved a deal with Honda to return as McLaren's engine supplier from 2015, which at the time was billed as an attempt to return to the uber-successful run of the late 1980s and early 1990s. This would continue after his exit (first as team CEO, a role Dennis resumed, then team principal), while McLaren also lost a major sponsor in Vodafone after 2013 that left its F1 cars appearing to lack backing.

Whitmarsh would go on to hold new roles, including CEO of the Ineos America's Cup team – before returning to F1 as group chief executive officer of Aston Martin Performance Technologies, a role he left in late 2024.

Dennis did not go back to running the McLaren F1 team as he previously had. Instead, he installed the former Lotus team principal, Eric Boullier, as racing director, while remaining in his McLaren Group roles. But Dennis's issues with his fellow owners were not over.

In late 2014, by which time Dennis had followed through on a plan initially begun under Whitmarsh and sensationally re-signed Alonso, by now racing for Ferrari, even bigger developments at the very top of McLaren were in motion.

Dennis had agreed with his fellow shareholders – at this stage the Bahrain royal family's Mumtalakat investment fund owned 50 per cent of the McLaren Group, having first taken on 30 per cent of the McLaren F1 team backed in 2007, with Dennis and Ojjeh owning 25 per cent each – that he could gain majority control if he could find new investors.

Nearly two years later, however, this had not happened. A deal Dennis thought he had secured with a Chinese consortium apparently worth £1.65 billion fell through. In the meantime,

ABOVE: Jenson Button, Whitmarsh and Sergio Pérez (all centre), lead McLaren's celebrations of the 50th anniversary of the team's founding at the 2013 Italian GP.

CLASH OF THE TITANS 117

ABOVE: Fernando Alonso in action for McLaren at the 2015 Japanese GP – a race where the Spaniard would castigate Honda for the poor performance of its Formula 1 engine.

Honda's first attempt at a turbo F1 engine in 27 years had been an embarrassing failure for the manufacturer and McLaren.

Its F1 results nosedived. From finishing third in 2012, it had slipped to fifth (twice) in the final years of its Mercedes customer deal and in 2015 finished ninth of the ten teams – its lowest constructors' ranking since 1980.

For Dennis, a showdown was coming. In November 2016, he sought an injunction from the High Court of England and Wales to prevent his fellow directors from suspending him. This failed and, with Dennis's contract with McLaren concluding in January 2017, his 36-year stint running the organization was over.

He stepped down from his positions, saying, "I am disappointed that the representatives of TAG and Mumtalakat, the other main shareholders in McLaren, have forced through this decision to place me on gardening leave, despite the strong warnings from the rest of the management team about the potential consequences of their actions on the business".

He added. "The grounds they have stated are entirely spurious; my management style is the same as it has always been and is one that has enabled McLaren to become an automotive and technology group that has won 20 Formula 1 world championships and grown into an £850-million-a-year business.

In June 2017, Dennis sold his shareholdings in McLaren Technology Group and McLaren Automotive for £275million and relinquished his directorships of both entities. A new era at McLaren was truly underway.

BELOW: Ron Dennis enacting Whitmarsh's plan to re-sign Fernando Alonso (left) was considered a bold strategy given the pair's difficult relationship at McLaren in 2007.

A NEW
START

CASTORE
android
DELL
Technologies
McLaren
FORMULA 1 TEAM
OKX
GRID ACCESS

THE HEIR:
ZAK BROWN

> "We'd become Darth Vader and I wanted us to be Luke Skywalker."

How McLaren changed in the years following Ron Dennis's exit. His successor as Formula 1 team boss, American marketeer Zak Brown, is an irrepressible character. The quote above was spoken in McLaren's giant motorhome in the F1 paddock at the 2024 Italian Grand Prix, painted papaya orange – in contrast to the imposing silver of his predecessor's era – simply because Brown is a McLaren fan.

The day after these words were uttered, McLaren drivers Oscar Piastri and Lando Norris fought for the race victory at Monza – the latter in championship contention and the first McLaren driver to be so since Lewis Hamilton back in 2010. The nadir of the final years of Dennis's reign finally seemed a mere memory.

OPPOSITE: Zak Brown has overseen a resurgence in McLaren's F1 fortunes.

"They were," Brown said in response to the suggestion that the boardroom showdowns through the final months of Dennis's time were dramatic. "I was there."

"The shareholders ultimately had a dispute and it was going to come down to one entity going to need to buy out the other. Because it was clear at that point it was no longer a harmonious relationship and seemed unrepairable."

But Brown claimed he entered the story of McLaren at Dennis's invitation as 2016 wore on.

By this point, Brown was nearly 45. He had started out hoping to make it as an F1 racer himself in the mid- to late-1980s. During McLaren's famously dominant 1988 season, he "fell in love with" the team and Ayrton Senna in particular. Brown won races throughout his time as a go-kart and junior single seater racer and rose as high as competing in the prestigious British Formula 3 series that Senna had won in 1983, as well as IndyCar's Indy Lights series on the other side of the Atlantic. This was 1994, but the following year Brown really started on the journey that led him to running McLaren's F1 squad.

His grand prix driver dream would never be realized – although Brown continued to race on for years, mainly in GT sportscar racing – but in 1995 he started a company that would lead him to the pinnacle of motor racing via another route.

Brown founded Just Marketing, which arranged sponsorship deals for motorsport teams and championships. This started out "of the necessity to just make a living", as well as to continue funding his professional racing ambitions. These finally ended in 2000, but in the meantime, Brown had realized "if I wasn't limited to just selling my own career, I could maybe turn it into something".

"I had no idea it was going to turn into what it did, which was ultimately the world's largest motorsports [sponsorship] agency," he continued.

"I sold the majority of it in 2008 but stayed on as CEO. And then in 2013, we sold the whole thing to Chime Communications, which was a London PLC. They then absorbed the business, put me in as group CEO [of the business then known as CSM] and I ran out my contractual period."

As Dennis was ultimately failing to acquire the funding to buy out his fellow McLaren owners, Brown admitted "Ron had been pursuing me". At the same time, the wider F1 world was changing significantly too, and this nearly altered Brown's career path massively once again.

Liberty Media had taken over the company that owned the championship's commercial rights, Formula One Management, and was starting to flesh out its vision for how F1 would subsequently change. This began with installing its own senior management group to lead FOM after former supremo Bernie Ecclestone was sidelined. Chase Carey was installed as F1 CEO, with Brown heavily linked with the role of commercial

BELOW: McLaren's difficult start to the 2017 Formula 1 season with the MCL32 led Brown and co to end the team's arrangement to run Honda engines.

ABOVE: Jenson Button makes a one-off reappearance for McLaren in Formula 1 at the 2017 Monaco GP, replacing Fernando Alonso, who was competing in the Indy 500.

boss. But with, as he put it, "a view to doing the big boy job at some point".

In late September 2016, Brown resigned as CSM CEO and was poised to join FOM, until McLaren came calling. As a result of "a prolonged wait" to find out the result of FOM's hiring process, Dennis and McLaren had come into the picture. Brown said he was left with "the opportunity to go to either Formula 1 or McLaren" and "ultimately picked McLaren because I felt it gave me the thrill of deal making, which I love".

"But what McLaren then also had was going racing," he added. "And I haven't looked back since."

Indeed, first as executive director of the McLaren Technology Group, Brown made an impact by reviving

McLaren's iconic papaya orange livery on its 2017 F1 car. This decision made headlines, as Dennis had resisted changing the team's colours even after Mercedes had departed as co-owner, much to the frustration of many McLaren supporters.

"That was what the fans wanted," Brown explained. "The car was dark [in 2015 and 2016], we weren't a very inclusive team, we weren't very approachable. But in today's day and age, I wanted the team to have a lot more inclusivity, be very warm, engaging, fan friendly."

But other wins were harder to find. Behind the scenes, Brown found a team where "there were a lot of ghosts being seen on the shop floor – morale was terrible". And so, he set off with a two-pronged strategy. First, to make a series of commercial deals that would increase sponsorship numbers

OPPOSITE: Fernando Alonso waves farewell at the 2018 Abu Dhabi GP – his final race for McLaren before he entered a sabbatical period from racing in Formula 1.

considerably (Brown claimed the team had 10 per cent of the sponsors it does in 2024 when he arrived), while at the same time learning and understanding the workforce to improve McLaren's working culture. With a happier squad and more money coming in, results would follow.

Except they did not. The 2017 F1 season had started with much expected from Honda's reshaped V6 turbo hybrid engine – particularly with more power promised from its internal combustion engine element. But McLaren's results were disastrous again, as the MCL32 car proved to be slow and unreliable.

"We could barely finish a race," Brown said of a year in which Fernando Alonso and Stoffel Vandoorne raced McLaren's first car without an MP4 moniker in 36 years.

Change was inevitable. McLaren ended its Honda partnership after just three years and did a new deal to run Renault customer units in F1 from 2018 – in part to convince Alonso to stay on board. The decision, Brown said, meant they "left a lot of money on the table". Honda soon teamed up with Red Bull and has since made good on the turbo hybrid programme that will switch to Aston Martin's team for 2026.

"But we felt, ultimately, it's a results-based business and if we weren't going to get results, then you're leaving this money on the table, but you're not going to get this money," Brown adds. "Your prize money, your sponsors aren't happy, and things of that nature."

Still, though, all was not right. McLaren's 2018 car – the MCL33 – was a regular points scorer, which was an improvement over its predecessor, but it was still far from leading a class that was by now dominated by its former partner Mercedes.

Alonso grew frustrated and opted to leave McLaren for an F1 sabbatical in 2019 – after Brown and co had allowed him

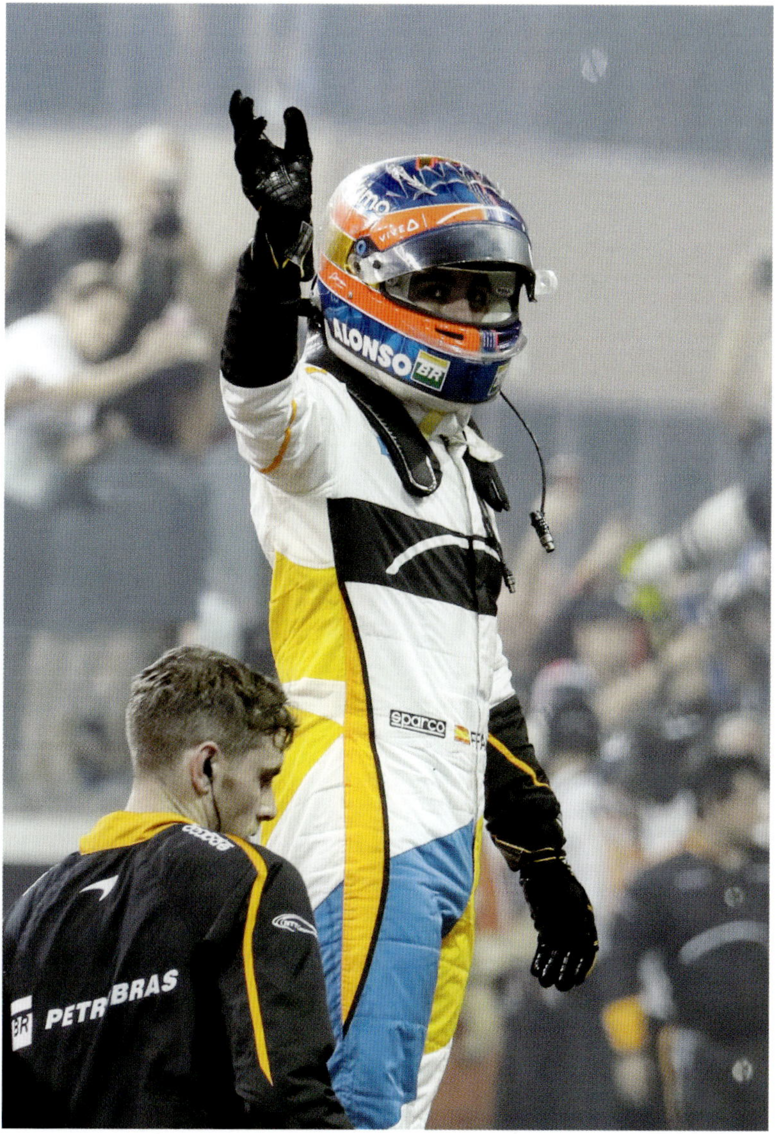
ALONSO
sparco
PETROBRAS

ABOVE: Lando Norris makes his Formula 1 debut at the 2019 Australian GP for McLaren. The Briton had previously been a junior driver for the team.

to make extra-curricular forays into IndyCar and sportscar racing's World Endurance Championship.

The problem was McLaren's F1 chassis was not as good as the team had previously assumed around Honda's engine issues.

"We were of the view," said Brown, "it was all their fault. And when we put another power unit in the back, we saw we were definitely not where we needed to be. It was a wake-up call."

Again, Brown's McLaren acted. He was by now working as McLaren Racing's CEO and reporting into the McLaren Group chairman role Paul Walsh has held since 2020, alongside the twin CEO of McLaren Automotive. These days, Mumtalakat owns 100 per cent of the McLaren Group, which owns 71 per cent of Racing, with the rest owned by MSP Sports Capital.

In mid-2018, Eric Boullier was ousted as McLaren's F1 racing director. The leadership of the team's technical department was also heavily revised. For 2019, Boullier was replaced by a new McLaren team principal: Andreas Seidl.

At the same time, big change had arrived on the driving front. To replace Alonso and former McLaren junior Vandoorne, another driver the team had invested in – Norris – and Carlos Sainz Jr came in. Via the latter, and with its car design now improving, McLaren scored its first podium since 2014 in the 2019 Brazilian Grand Prix.

Here the results began to pick up, as Brown and Seidl – a Le Mans-winning team principal for Porsche – also agreed a major investment programme was required at the McLaren Technology Centre. This meant building an expensive new wind tunnel critical to getting the best F1 car designs. By 2019's end, McLaren also had decided to do another engine deal and resume as a Mercedes customer from 2021.

BELOW: Carlos Sainz Jr's podium finish at the 2019 Brazilian GP was McLaren's first in F1 for five years. He was boosted to third after Mercedes' Lewis Hamilton was penalized.

ABOVE: McLaren returned to racing in the IndyCar championship in the United States for the 2020 season in partnership with the Arrow Schmidt Peterson Motorsports team.

OPPOSITE: Daniel Ricciardo ended McLaren's near nine-year F1 win drought with his emotional victory in the 2021 Italian race ahead of Lando Norris.

From scoring two more podiums with Norris and Sainz in 2020 – the year the team finished third in the constructors' championship, having made steady progress since being ninth again in 2017 – McLaren finally became an F1 race winner again in 2021. This came via Daniel Ricciardo, who had been signed to replace Sainz when the Spaniard joined Ferrari.

F1 then began a new technical rules era in 2022, with a move back to cars using the ground-effect principle as the main driver for aerodynamics. This was such a dramatic departure from the previous rules – and done because these types of cars can overtake each other more easily – it raised expectations that finally McLaren might vault its way back to challenging for F1 titles for the first time since 2008.

This was not to be at first. And when a major car upgrade package introduced at the 2022 French GP did not work as expected, Brown decided he had to act again regarding the team's leadership.

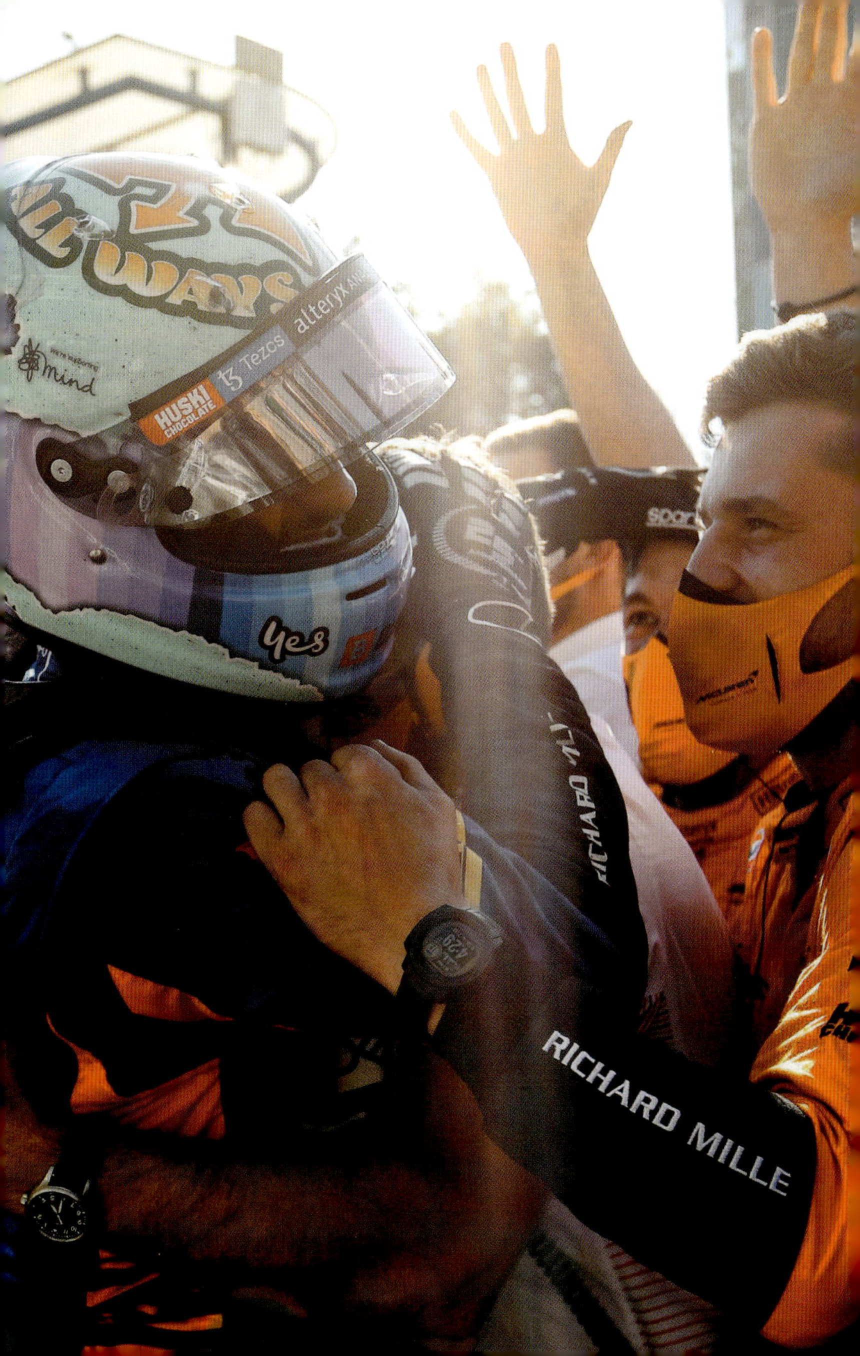
HUSKI CHOCOLATE
Tezos
alteryx
mind
yes
RICHARD MILLE

ABOVE: Brown would replace Andreas Seidl as McLaren's Formula 1 team principal with Italian engineer Andrea Stella ahead of the 2023 season.

"That can happen," Brown said. "What I didn't like was the lack of response, and urgency and concern, that it didn't work."

By this stage, Seidl had received an offer to head up Audi's new F1 programme from 2026 at the end of his McLaren contract. But Brown decided "'you can go now'" at the end of 2022 and then revived a plan he had originally had back in 2018. This was to make Andrea Stella – McLaren's latest racing director, albeit in a less senior position than Boullier – run the show. Stella had worked as a vital engineer to Michael Schumacher at Ferrari during the German driver's world title run in the early 2000s and held a similar role with Alonso before following him to McLaren in 2015.

"I actually wanted to appoint Andrea before we appointed Andreas," Brown revealed. "I wanted to promote Andrea, but he felt he wasn't ready yet. So, I brought in Andreas. That didn't work out, at all."

In Stella's first season as McLaren team boss in 2023, the squad began running Piastri as Norris's teammate. Ricciardo's results had been too inconsistent and the decision had been made the previous summer to pay him off from the rest of his contract. Piastri was so highly rated that McLaren had gone to court over his 2023 services, after it signed him from the Alpine squad where he had been a rising star.

The 2023 F1 season started with McLaren off the pace because of the previous year's design failings, but by mid-year the MCL37 was pushing the now-dominant-again Red Bull team for victories.

In 2024, further improvements to its car design package led to McLaren's first multi-win season in 12 years. Brown

BELOW: Lando Norris's impressive results contributed to the team deciding to replace Daniel Ricciardo with his compatriot Oscar Piastri for 2023.

OVERLEAF: Since 2022, McLaren has fielded a team in the all-electric Formula E championship. Here with Jake Hughes (centre) and René Rast.

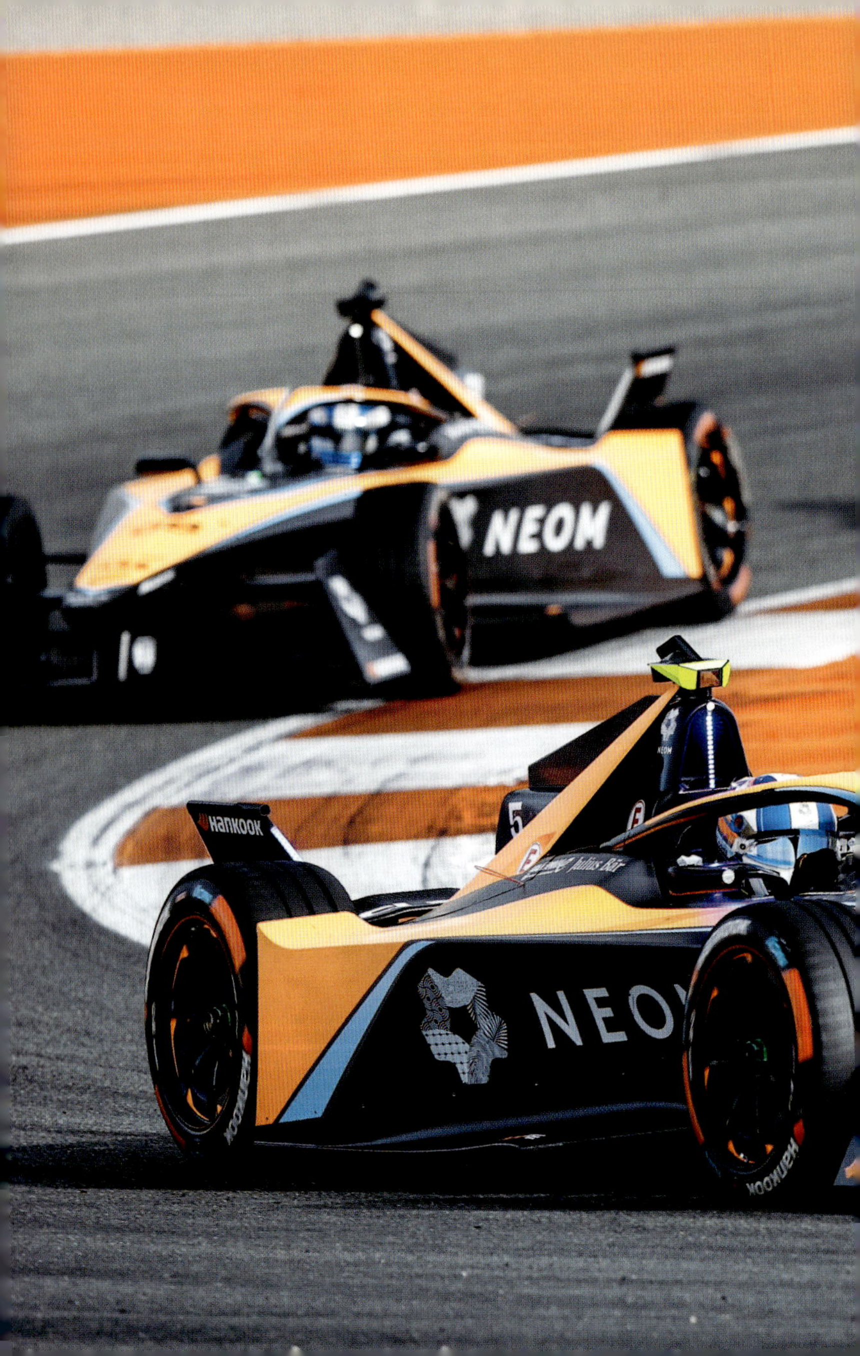
NEOM
Hankook
Julius Bär

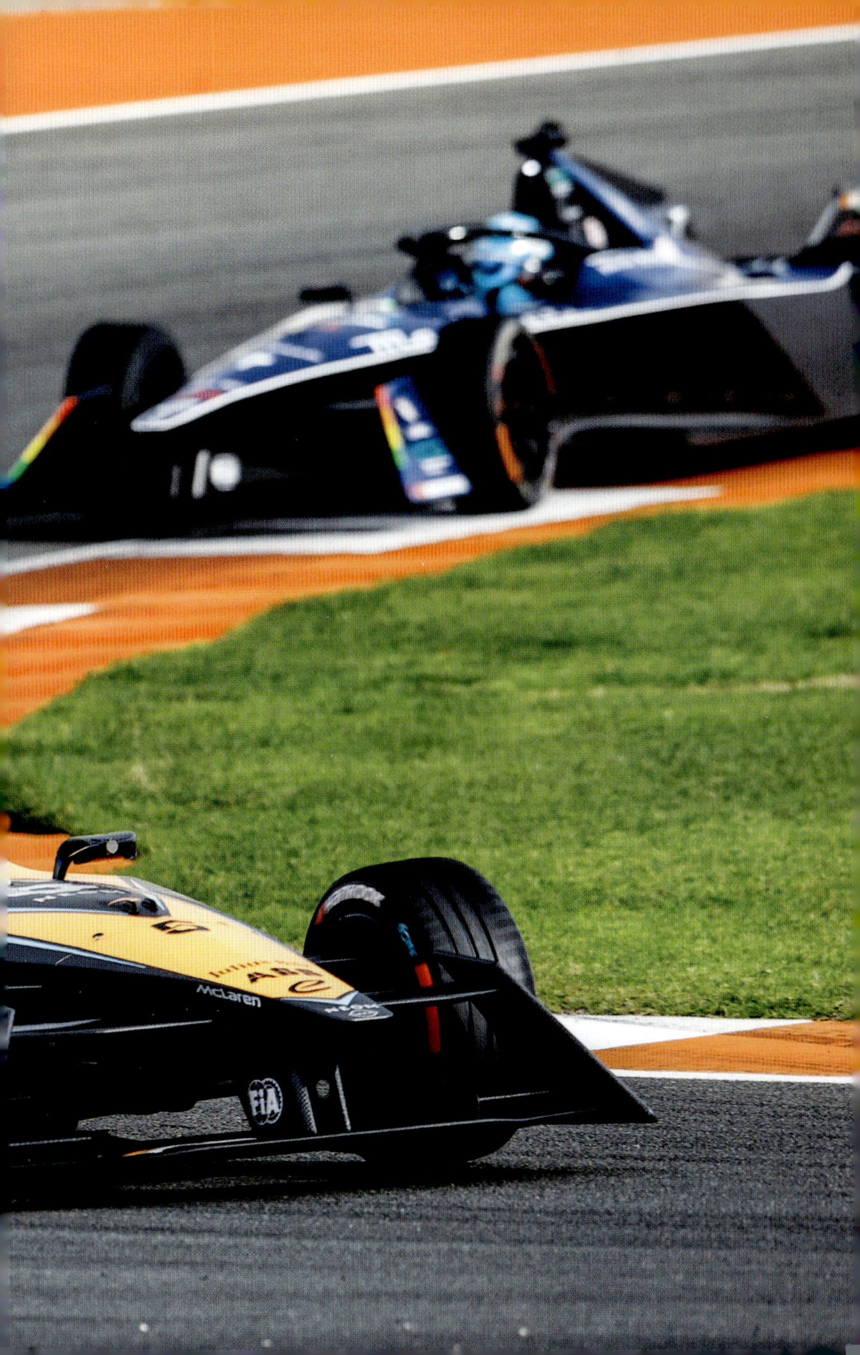
McLaren
FIA

credited Stella for "unleashing" talented engineers, such as aerodynamics chief Peter Prodromou – a former key colleague of Adrian Newey at both McLaren in the 1990s and Red Bull in the late-2000s to mid-2010s – with new responsibilities.

With McLaren now firmly on the up again, Brown has big hopes for its future, yet ones that evoke memories of the team's past achievements, as well as Bruce's own.

"Probably the one thing I'd like to get done here is get us in Le Mans," he explained. "And if we can, at one point, win Le Mans, F1's Monaco GP and the Indy 500 as one group, [that] would be cool. If we wanna get really greedy, it would be fun to do it all in one year."

But what would ending McLaren's long F1 title drought mean to Brown?

"Everything…"

BELOW: Lando Norris (left) and Oscar Piastri celebrate McLaren winning the 2024 Hungarian GP, which was the latter's first F1 grand prix victory.

OPPOSITE: Lando Norris crosses the finish line to win the 2024 Miami Grand Prix. It was the British driver's first Formula 1 victory after 110 GP starts.

138 A NEW START

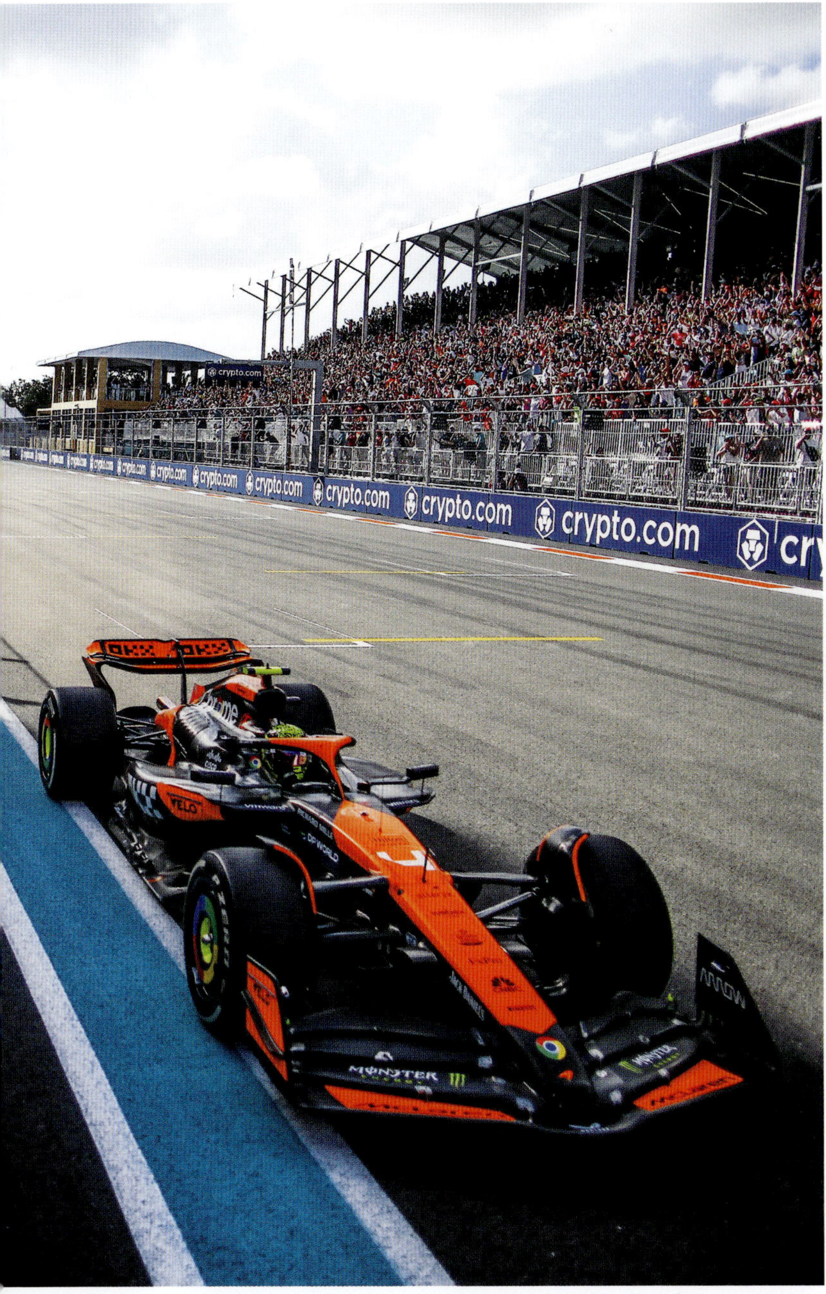
crypto.com
VELO

TRANSFORMATION COMPLETE

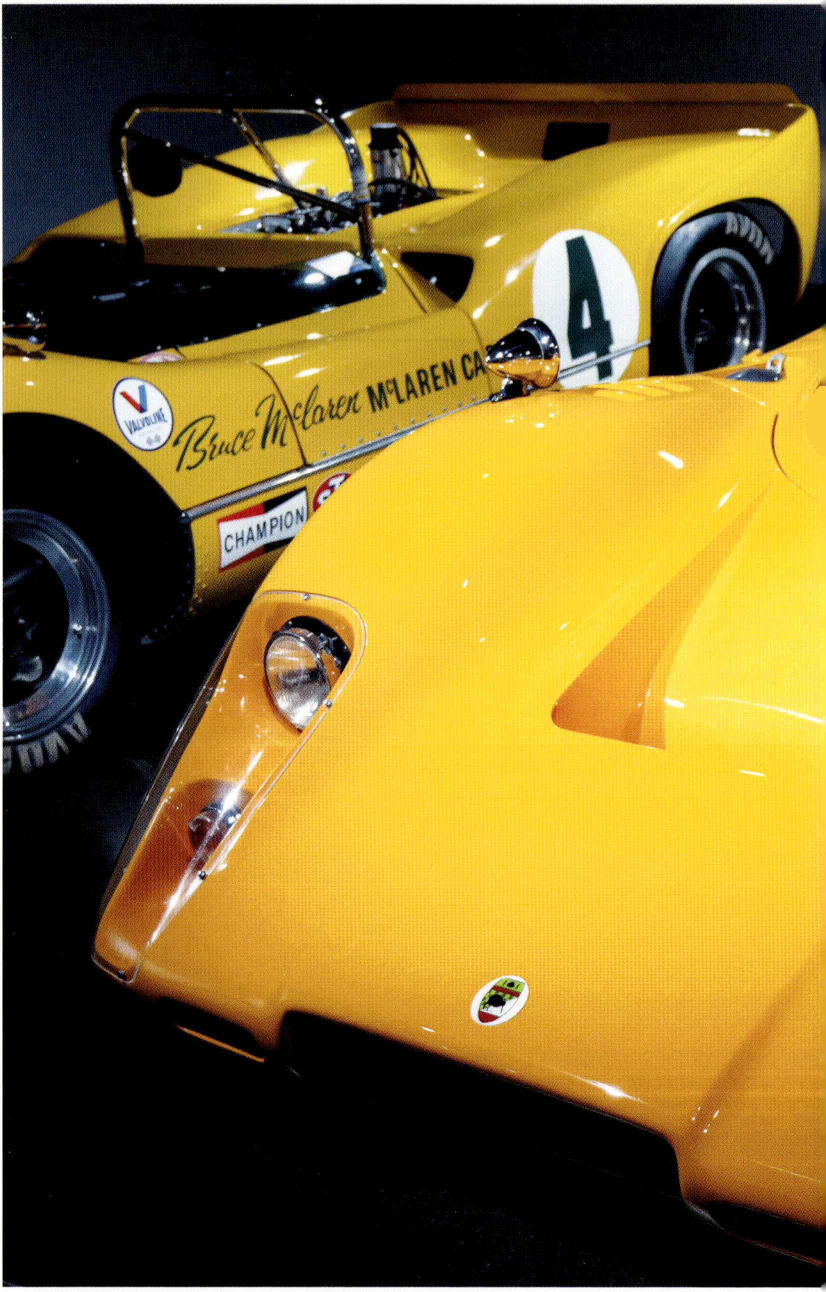
Bruce McLaren
McLAREN CA
4
VALVOLINE
CHAMPION

THE CARS:
AUTOMOTIVE

> The story of McLaren is not just about motorsport.
> Although these days it is active in a wider range of motor
> racing championships than it had been for a long swathe
> of its history, its Automotive road car production corps
> is world-renowned.

Tying these various strands together is the company's headquarters: the McLaren Technology Centre. Opened in 2004 after six years of construction on the site of a former ostrich farm, the MTC was designed by Wembley stadium architect Norman Foster. The impetus for this move was Ron Dennis wanting to improve overall efficiency within McLaren by providing staff with state-of-the art facilities in which to work.

The MTC moved the company and its Formula 1 race division from nearby Woking town's business park – following on from their previous factory site in Colnbrook. The MTC sits at 63,000m² – beside a man-made lake that dissipates heat from a wind tunnel below. A huge glass façade provides McLaren employees with views over the surrounding Surrey countryside, while in front of the lake a boulevard stretch of

OPPOSITE: The 1969 McLaren M6GT (right) was designed by Bruce.

TRANSFORMATION COMPLETE 143

the interior regularly hosts historic examples of McLaren's racing designs, just feet from where the current F1 racers are assembled and serviced.

In 2021, Zak Brown and his fellow senior managers authorized McLaren to make a £170 million sale and leaseback deal with the Global Net Lease company for the MTC, as the company faced serious cashflow issues during the COVID-19 pandemic.

"Why have all this money tied up in real estate?" Brown said at the time. "We're not a real estate company. We're a racing team and an automotive company."

The sprawling site includes the McLaren Production Centre. Also designed by Foster, and opened in 2011 by then UK prime minister David Cameron and featuring a subterranean walkway to connect with the MTC's main building, here the models from the McLaren Automotive range are assembled. Certain additional bodyshell parts are produced at a separate composites facility in Sheffield.

The history of McLaren's road car offerings can be traced back to Bruce's M6GT design. This was a "genuinely street legal road car" with "Can-Am cousins", according to McLaren biographer William Taylor, that Bruce designed himself in 1969. The project was ultimately shelved – bar the prototype built for Bruce to use and fettle as his personal car. Any ambitions he had for one day still selling the M6GT *en masse* died with him, but Denny Hulme later bought the prototype car and shipped it home to New Zealand.

In 1989, Dennis formed McLaren Cars from another related company – TAG McLaren Research & Development LTD. This produced the world-famous McLaren F1.

Designed by Gordon Murray and Peter Stevens, it was at the time the world's fastest production car, with a launch at the 1993 Monaco GP. Featuring an unusual three-seat cockpit and central driving position, the F1 was the first supercar with an all-carbon fibre monocoque, which was allied to active aerodynamics to achieve enhanced corner handling around what was at the time conceived as the highest power-to-weight ratio of any production car.

The F1 cost £634,500 at the time of its release (£1,323,000 today) and had a top speed of 240mph. It was noted as being able to reach 150mph quicker than most sportscars of the time could reach 60mph by *Autocar* magazine. Its 627bhp came

BELOW: McLaren's F1 supercar was launched at the 1993 Monaco GP. It featured a rare three-seat cockpit layout and was designed by Gordon Murray and Peter Stevens.

ABOVE: The Kokusai Kaihatsu-entered McLaren F1 GTR wins the 1995 Le Mans 24 Hours. It was driven by Yannick Dalmas, Masanori Sekiya and JJ Lehto.

from a BMW-designed V12 engine. Just 70 F1s were made (including prototypes), with extremely limited edition F1 LM and F1 GT varieties built in 1996 and 1997 respectively.

In 1995, a McLaren F1 GTR (which inspired the LM edition) entered by the Kokusai Kaihatsu team won the Le Mans 24 Hours endurance sportscar race – 29 years after Bruce's triumph in the same legendary event for Ford. McLaren had only decided to adapt the F1 for racing to boost flagging sales and was not confident the modified design could even last a 24-hour test.

Through this success, McLaren can claim the 'Triple Crown of Motorsport' – a prestigious title awarded to those who have won the F1 world title, Indianapolis 500 and 24 Hours of Le Mans (an alternative interpretation swaps the F1 championship for victory in the Monaco GP). The only racer to lay claim to a Triple Crown was Bruce's contemporary, Graham Hill, with the accolade generally only applying to drivers. Although McLaren's F1 titles and 15 Monaco GP wins (the most of any team, with five coming via Ayrton Senna) certainly count towards such a consideration, the unofficial, semi-works status of the Kokusai Kaihatsu squad (which was nevertheless put together by McLaren) also detracts from the company's claim.

But there can be no denying the McLaren F1's impact on the supercar sphere upon its release. It was declared "not simply the fastest mid-engined supercar ever built, but the most practical (it had space for luggage in its flanks)" by renowned magazine *Motor Sport*. Its celebrity owners include Rowan Atkinson and Jay Leno.

For 16 years, however, the F1 remained McLaren's sole road car offering, as the McLaren Cars division lay effectively dormant between 1994 and 2010. Not that this stopped the marque's name from appearing in the automotive business in the decade following the F1's release.

As part of its close collaboration with Mercedes, the two companies joined forces on a Grand Touring supercar – with a far greater production volume than that of the F1. This became

BELOW: The Mercedes-Benz SLR McLaren was launched at the 2003 IAA Frankfurt motor show, as McLaren and Mercedes took their partnership into road cars.

BELOW: The Mercedes-Benz SLR McLaren Stirling Moss was around 200kg lighter than the SLR Roadster and featured a longer, lower nose, no roof or windows.

the Mercedes-Benz SLR McLaren, which was introduced to the world at the 2003 IAA Frankfurt motor show. The SLR – 'Sport-Leicht-Rennsport' or 'Sport-Light-Racing' – honoured Mercedes' success in the 1955 Mille Miglia 1000-mile road race that went from Brescia to Rome and back again.

Powered by a supercharged 5.4 litre AMG Mercedes V8, the SLR produced 626bhp. It could do 0–62mph in 3.8 seconds, 0–125 mph in 10.6 seconds, and had a top speed of 207mph. The car was mid-engined, but to achieve the stated aim of a 49:51 front to rear weight distribution, it was placed ahead of the driver and as far back as possible. The bonnet was made long enough to incorporate this aspect, along with side exit exhaust pipes.

Here came McLaren's main contribution – producing a dedicated carbon composite tub that had high torsional rigidity, as inspired by its many racing designs since the MP4/1. The SLR also featured a separate carbon fibre crash structure that was styled to look like the nose cone of an F1 racer. The SLR's aerodynamics were derived from McLaren's motorsport exploits, too. It featured a flat floor that combined with a rear diffuser to add downforce, with an initial asking price of £315,000 (£560,000 in 2024). As the SLR's production run went on, Mercedes tasked McLaren with producing a soft-top Roadster version, plus a final iteration – the SLR Stirling Moss. This was a 75-model run of a special version of the SLR, which nodded to famed 1950s–1960s racing driver Moss's Mille Miglia success for Mercedes.

The value of the Mercedes SLR collaboration was measured in different ways to just total car sales and income. McLaren claimed ahead of its milestone relaunch of McLaren Cars in 2010 – rebranded as McLaren Automotive that year – that having been able to produce a maximum of three F1 road cars a month during its production run, the experience gained with the SLR meant that it was then capable of making up to four cars a day.

With the expansion of the MTC to include greater road car production facilities just around the corner, McLaren announced in 2010 that, after five years of planning, the car sales from the Automotive arm would "support the long-term future of McLaren and our people".

McLaren Automotive's first car was the MP4-12C. Named in homage to McLaren's old F1 car designations, it was released in 2011.

Dennis said it realized "a long-held dream of mine to launch high-performance sports cars that set new standards in the industry". The MP4-12C is powered by a bespoke McLaren-built V8 twin-turbo engine that put out 600hp. It was followed by a Spider roadster version in 2012, after the MP4 part of the name had been dropped.

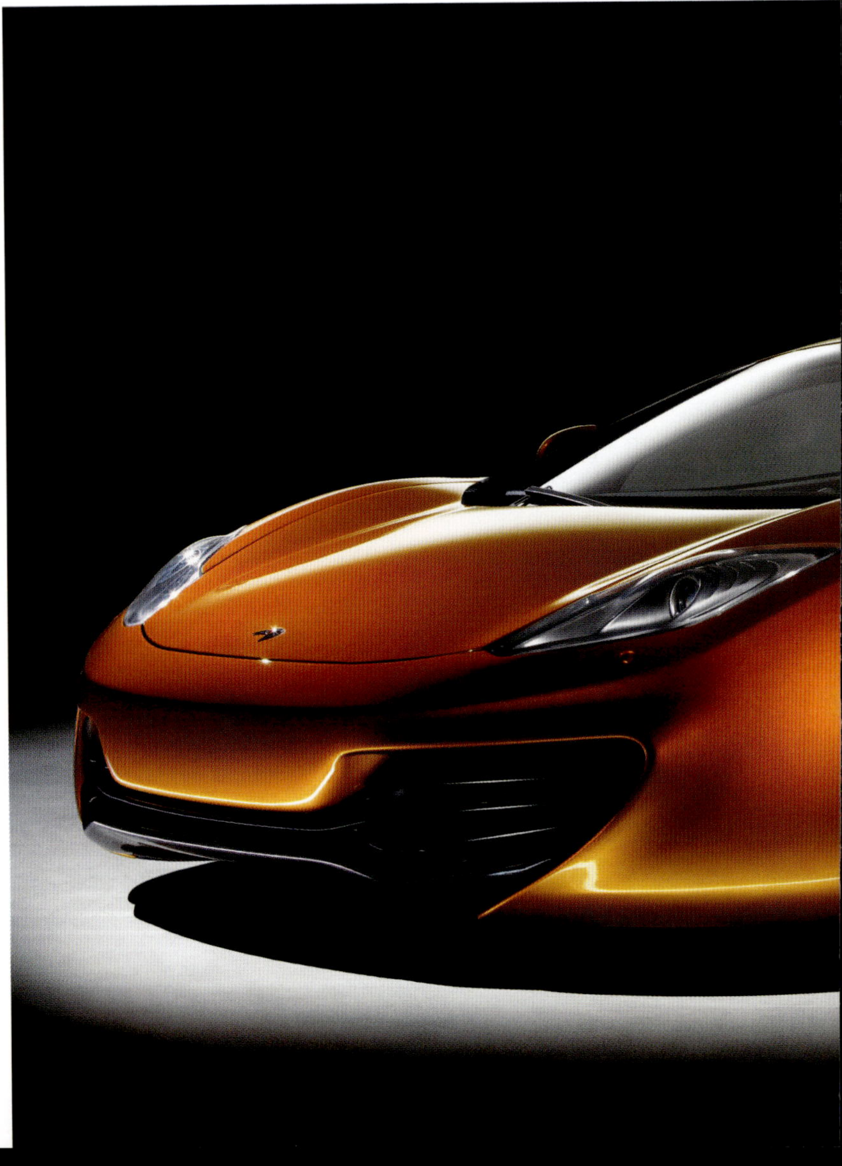

BELOW: The MP4-12C was McLaren Automotive's first design when it launched in 2011 and its name referenced McLaren's old F1 car model designations.

BELOW: The McLaren P1 on display at the Geneva Motor Show in 2013. The model, of which 375 were produced, was McLaren's first high-performance hybrid supercar.

In 2013, McLaren released its first high-performance hybrid supercar, the P1, which debuted at the previous year's Paris Motor Show. This twin-turbo engine car, of which 375 were made, combined with an electric motor to produce 903bhp and a top speed of 217mph. Next came 2014's 650S. Its S stands for 'Sport', with coupé and Spider roadster models offered from the start of its production run. The 650 refers to its calculated horsepower output (641bhp), as do the names of similar later McLaren models.

By 2015, McLaren had structured Automotive's offering so that it covered three distinct lines: the Sports, Super, and Ultimate series.

The 2015-released 675LT echoed the 'longtail' design added to the F1 GTR back in 1997, while in 2017 the McLaren Senna was named after the celebrated F1 champion. In 2018, the McLaren Speedtail was introduced – considered something of a successor to the McLaren F1 because of its similar three-seat cockpit layout.

In 2019, McLaren altered Automotive's structure again to incorporate a fourth offering: GT. The McLaren GT was then released that year. Since 2012, certain McLaren designs – starting with the MP4-12C GT3 – had also been adapted for use in the GT category of sportscar racing via the company's dedicated McLaren GT division. In 2024, the GT's successor – the GTS – was introduced to McLaren's fleet.

The McLaren Elva of 2020 pays homage to the deal with the now-defunct British manufacturer that Bruce made in the early days of the company's existence. Today, McLaren offers the Solus GT, which also traces the Ultimate series lineage back to the F1 road car. This track-only car was originally designed as a concept in the *Gran Turismo* video game series.

But the McLaren name can also be found elsewhere. McLaren Applied – first formed as McLaren Applied Technologies as part of an amalgamation of various subsidiary companies in 2003 – is actually no longer owned by the McLaren Group. The company, which since 2008 has supplied

BELOW: A McLaren GT at the 2019 Goodwood Festival of Speed. A dedicated GT division has adapted McLaren supercars for use in sportscar racing since 2012.

ABOVE: A McLaren Elva on display at the 2020 Salon Privé Concours d'Elegance event held at Blenheim Palace in England in the year it was released.

the standard ECU (electronic control unit) that processes all the data and command functions on all F1 cars, plus other components made for teams across the current grid, has been owned by the Greybull Capital investment company since 2021.

Throughout its history, McLaren Applied worked on projects including performance management systems for Team GB's sailing, rowing, canoeing and cycling squads at the 2012 Olympics, improved production efficiency for pharmaceutical giant GSK, and made the S-Works+ McLaren Venge for bicycle company Specialized. Separately, the McLaren group also had a short-lived partnership with the Bahrain-Victorious professional cycling team.

McLaren is now active in new and emerging motorsport disciplines as well. After the Applied division had produced the spec electric motor for the first season of the all-electric Formula E championship, and the spec battery for its Gen 2 era between 2018–2022, McLaren entered its own team in the series. Since 2022, McLaren has also fielded a team in the related Extreme E off-road electric racing series.

And in bringing McLaren's racing story to intertwine again in a manner of which Bruce would no doubt approve, the company recently opted to rejoin the American racing scene, where it enjoyed so much success right back at its roots in the 1960s and 1970s.

After two dedicated attempts to win the Indy 500 with former F1 driver Fernando Alonso (in 2017 in collaboration with the Andretti Autosport organization), Brown's McLaren Racing re-entered Indycar racing full-time in 2020. It partnered with the Sam Schmidt Motorsports squad at the time, then wielded the controlling stake in the team, with Brown acting as its chairman, since 2022.

Papaya orange liveries are racing on both sides of the Atlantic and all around the world as the 2020s unfurl. McLaren's story continues, exactly as Bruce had begun it.

BELOW: A McLaren Solus GT is presented at the 2024 Goodwood Festival of Speed. Only 25 models will be produced, with the car originally a gaming concept.

INDEX

(Key: *italic* refers to photos/captions)

A

Abu Dhabi Grand Prix *128*
Adamich, Andrea de 68
Aintree *13*
Alfa Romeo 68
Alonso, Fernando 13, 80–1, *81*, 97, 105, 106–7, *118*, *126*, 128, *128*, 131, 155
AMG Mercedes 149
Anderson, Gary *40*
Andretti Autosport 155
Andretti, Michael 61, 93
Argentine Grand Prix 14, 36, 38
Arrow Schmidt Peterson *132*
Aston Martin Performance Technologies 116
Atkinson, Rowan 147
Austin-Healey 31
Austin Seven 14
Australian Grand Prix *43*, 88, 93, 97, *108*, *130*
Autocar 145
Autosport 9, 18, 25, 61, 86, 94, 112

B

Bahrain-Victorious 154
Barnard, John 53, 59, 69–70
Belgian Grand Prix 23, *23*, 29, 38, *66*
Benetton 67
Berger, Gerhard 87, *88*
Blenheim Palace *154*
Blundell, Sir Denis 25, *93*
BMW 52, 66, 69, 146
BMW ProCar M1 50, 52, 55
Boullier, Eric 116, 130–1
Brabham 49, 53
Brabham, Jack 10, 11, 13–14, *13*, 16, 17, 49
Brawn GP 111–12, *112*
Brawn, Ross 111
Brazilian Grand Prix *36*, *58*, 70, 88, *88*, 98, 108, 114, *116*, 131, *131*
BRDC International Trophy 14
British Aerospace (BAe) 107
British Grand Prix *13*, *28*, 36, 39, 40, *50*, 55, *56*, *98*
British Racing Motors (BRM) 22, *67*
Brown, Creighton 51
Brown, Zak 123–35, 144, 155
Bruce McLaren Motor Racing Ltd 17
Brundle, Martin *76*
Button, Jenson 80, *108*, *112*, 114, *115*, *117*, *126*

C

Cameron, David 144
Can-Am 22, 25, *25*, *30*, *31*, 34, 35–6, 40, 69
Canadian Grand Prix 36, 38, 97
Carey, Chase 125
Chapman, Colin 22, 53
Chime Communications/ CSM 125–6
Chinese Grand Prix 97, *112*
Chipstead Motor Group 48
Chrysler 76
Clark, Jim 25
Colnbrook factory 34, 143
Cooper 10–14, *11*, *13*, 17, 18, *25*, 33, 48, *49*
 'Lowline Cooper' 14
 T60 *14*
 T66 17
Cooper, Charles 11, 16, 20
Cooper, John 11, 20
Cooper, John and Charles 11, 16
Cosworth 22, 67, *68*, *69*
Coughlan, Mike 106
Coulthard, David 79, 93
covid-19 144

D

Dalmas, Yannick *146*
Dennis, Ron 40, *43*, 47–61, *49*, *52*, *59*, *60*, 65–6, 69–70, 73–9, 86, 88, 90, *90*, 93–8, *96*, 105–8, 115–19, *118*, 123–8, 143, 149
Donington *50*, 89, *89*
Donohue, Mark 35
'Driver to Europe' scholarship 10
Dutch Grand Prix 25, 29

156 INDEX

E

Eagle 22
Ecclestone, Bernie 125
ECU (electronic control unit) 154
Ecuador-Marlboro 50
Elizabeth II 48
Elva Cars 18
European Grand Prix 89, *89*
EVs (electric vehicles) *135*, 154–5
Extreme E 155

F

Federation Internationale de l'Automobile (FIA) 106–7, 107, 108, 111
Ferrari 56, 87, 90, 94, 96, 106, 117, 132, 134
Ferrari, Enzo 65
Firestone 18
Fittipaldi, Emmerson 36, *36*, 38, 68, *69*
Ford 18, 18–20, *18*, 21–2, *53*, 55, 59, 65, 67, *68*, *69*, *73*, 146
Formula 2 10, *11*, 49, 50, 69
Formula 3 52, 124
Formula E *135*, 154
Formula One Management (FOM) 125
Formula One Teams' Association (FOTA) 111
Foster, Norman 143, 144
Frankfurt Motor Show *147*, 149
French Grand Prix *79*, 132
FW14B 89

G

Galli, Nanni 68
garagiste 65, 66
Gen2 cars 154–5
Geneva Motor Show *152*
German Grand Prix 10, *11*, 39, 55
Gethin, Peter 29
Global Net Lease 144
Goodwood Festival of Speed *153*, 155
Goodyear 35
Gran Turismo 153
Greybull Capital 154
GSK 154
Gurney, Dan 29

H

Haas-Lola *43*
Häkkinen, Mika 61, 79, 85–99, *90*, *93*, *94*
Hamilton, Lewis 85–99, *96*, *98*, 105, 106–7, 108, *111*, 112–15, *112*, 123, *131*
Haug, Norbert *59*
Hill, Graham 146
Hogan, John 50, 53
Honda 55, 56–60, 67, 73–6, 73, 80, *80*, 86, 116, *118*, *125*, 128, 130
Hughes, Jake *135*
Hulme, Denny 17, 22, 23, 29, *30*, *32*, 34, 35, 38, *67*, 144
Hungarian Grand Prix 13, 98, 106, *106*, *111*, *138*
Hunt, James 38–40, *38*, *39*, 68

I

ICI 51
Indianapolis 500 (Indy 500) 21, 29, 30, *34*, 35, *126*
Indy Lights series 124
IndyCar 124, 130, *132*, 155
International Grand Prix Association 10
Italian Grand Prix 39, *40*, *49*, 81, 86, *117*, 123, *132*

J

Japanese Grand Prix *39*, 56, *56*, 73, 86–7, *86*, *94*, *118*
Jarama *38*
Jerez 94
Just Marketing 124

K

Kerr, Phil 14, 33–4, 36–7
Kimbolton *96*
Kokusai Kaihatsu 146, *146*

L

Laguna Seca track *30*, *31*
Lamborghini 76
Lauda, Niki 39, 52, *52*, *53*, 55, 70
Le Mans 24 Hours 9, 18, *18*, 138, 146
Lehto, JJ *146*
Leno, Jay 147
Levin 17
Liberty Media 125

INDEX 157

Lola 34
Long Beach *52*
Lotus 22, 40, 53, *68*, 73, 85–6, 86, 90

M

McLaren Applied/ McLaren Applied Technologies 153–4
McLaren Automotive 118, 130, 144, 149, *151*, 152
McLaren, Bruce 9–25, *9*, *11*, *14*, 25, *25*, 29, *29*, 30, 33, 34, 47, 65–7, *66*, 138, *143*, 146, 153, 155
McLaren Cars 144, 147, 149
675LT 152
M1B 22
M2A 18
M2B 20, 21, *21*
M4B 22
M6A 22, 34–5
M6GT *143*, 144
M7A 22
M8D 25, *25*, *30*
M9A 23
M16 35
M23 68, *69*
M26 40
MCL32 *125*, 128
MCL33 128
MP4 128
MP4/1 40, 53, 55, 70, 149
MP4/2 70
MP4/4 56, *73*, 86–7
MP4/5 73, 87
MP4/8 67, 76, 89
MP4/9 *76*, 78, 93
MP4-12C 149, *151*
MP4/13 94
MP4-24 *106*
MP4-26 *112*
MP4-27 112
P1 152, *152*
Solus *155*
Speedtail 152
McLaren Group 55, 108, 112, 117, 130, 153–4
McLaren International 40, 55
McLaren, Patty (née Broad) 14, *14*
McLaren Production Centre (MPC) 144
McLaren Racing 130, 155
McLaren Senna 152
McLaren Technology Centre (MTC) 131, 143–4, 149
McLaren Technology Group 118, 126
Maddock, Owen 14
Magnussen, Jan 96
Mansell, Nigel 79, 89
Marlboro 36, 38, 40, 50, 51–4, 79, 90
Mayer, Teddy 17, 29–43, *29*, *39*, *40*, *43*, 47, 65, 69
Mayer, Timmy 17, 18, 21, 30–1, 32
Mercedes *59*, 79, 79–80, *79*, 98, *98*, 108, *108*, 111, 114–15, 118, 131, *131*, 147, *147*, 149
Mercedes-Benz SLR McLaren *147*, 148
Mercedes-Benz SLR McLaren Stirling Moss *148*, *149*
Mercedes FO 110 *79*
Mexican Grand Prix 23, 49
Miami Grand Prix *138*
Mille Miglia 149
Monaco Grand Prix 16, *21*, *69*, 70, *70*, *126*, 138, 144, *145*, 146
Monza 39, *49*, 123
Mosley, Max 107
Moss, Stirling 149
Motor Sport 147
MSP Sports Capital 130
Mumtalakat 117, 118
Murray, Gordon 53, 58–9, 144, *145*

N

New Zealand Grand Prix 10, 17

Newey, Adrian 94, 108, 138
Nicholson McLaren Engines 68
Norris, Lando 81, 98, 123, *130*, 131, 132, *132*, 135, *135*, *138*
Nürburgring 10, 39
Nye, Doug 10, 14, 33, 36, 48, 50, 52

O

OAPEC Oil Crisis (1973) 50
Offenhauser 35
Ojjeh, Mansour 55, 70, 115, 117
Olympics, London 2012 154
Osella 52
Overtaking Working Group (OWG) 108, 111

P

Pacific Grand Prix 96
Paul Ricard track 93
Penkse M16B 35
Penske-Porsche 35
Pérez, Sergio 114, *115*, *117*
Peterson, Ronnie 40
Peugeot 78–9, 93
Piastri, Oscar 81, 98, 123, 135, *135*, *138*
Porsche *53*, 55, 69–70, 70, 131

158 INDEX

Porsche 917 35
Portuguese Grand
  Prix *90*, 93
Prodromou, Peter 138
Project 3 50
Project 4 *43*, *50*,
  51–3, 55, *55*
Prost, Alain 40, 55–8,
  55, *56*, 70, *70*, 73,
  86–9, *88*

R

Räikkönen, Kimi 79,
  94, 96–7
Rast, René *135*
Red Bull 86, 98, 112,
  112, 128, 135, 138
Renault 55, 69, 80–1,
  81, 97, 128
Rev-Em Racing team
  30
Revson, Peter 30, *31*,
  34, 35–6
Reynolds Metals
  Company 34
Ricciardo, Daniel 81,
  132, *132*, 135, *135*
Rindt, Jochen 49, *49*
road cars 48, 59, 66,
  114, 143–55, *147*,
  148, 149, 153
Robson, Dave 97
Rondel Racing
  49–50, 50
Rosa, Pedro de la 106
Rutherford, Johnny
  35–6

S

Sebring 13, *13*
Seidl, Andreas 131,
  134, *134*
Sekiya, Masanori *146*
Senna, Ayrton 55–6,
  56, *58*, 60–1, *60*,
  67, 73–6, *73*, 78,
  85–99, *86*, *88*, *89*,
  90, 124, 147, 152
Serenissima 21
Silverstone *56*
Singapore Grand Prix
  98, 106
Smith, Bill 30
South African Grand
  Prix 32, 36, *67*
Spa-Francorchamps
  23, *66*
Spanish Grand Prix
  22, *38*, 39
sponsorship 36, 53,
  116, 127
Spygate 97, 106–7,
  112
Stella, Andrea 134–8,
  134
Stevens, Peter 144,
  145
Stewart, Jackie 23
Stuck, Hans-Joachim
  50
Suzuka 87–8, *94*
Swedish Grand Prix
  36

T

TAG Heuer *53*, 55
TAG McLaren
  Research &
  Development LTD
  144
Tambay, Patrick *43*
Tasman Series *16*,
  17, 32
Taylor, William 53,
  78, 144
Techniques d'Avant
  Garde (TAG) 55,
  70, 118
Texaco 36
Toleman 85
Toyota 111–12
Triple Crown of
  Motorsport 146
Trundle, Neil 49
Tyrrell Formula
  Junior 31
Tyrrell, Ken 30

U

Ulster Austin Seven
  10
United States Grand
  Prix *13*, 29–30, *30*,
  43, *52*, 98
USA Formula Junior
  30

V

Vandoorne, Stoffel
  128, 131

Vettel, Sebastian
  112–14, *112*
Villeneuve, Jacques
  94
Vodafone 116

W

Walsh, Paul 130
Watkins Glen track
  43
Watson, John 40, 55
West 79
Whitmarsh, Martin
  60–1, 80, 96, 98,
  105–19, *105*, *108*,
  116
Williams 53, 55,
  58–61, *60*, 67, 70,
  73–6, 89–90, *90*,
  111
Willmott, Wally 17
World Endurance
  Championship 130

Y

Yardley 36
Young, Eoin 18

Z

Zandvoort *25*

CREDITS

The publishers would like to thank the following sources for their kind permission to reproduce the pictures in this book.

ALAMY STOCK PHOTO: CJM Photography 153; P Cox 152; DPPI Media 133; Foto Arena LTDA 131; Goddard Archive 46; Malcolm Haines 154; Horizon International Images 56; Motoring Picture Library 68; Motorsport Archive Images 96; James Moy 100-101, 114, 118; ZUMA Press, Inc. 132

GETTY IMAGES: Ulrich Baumgarten 147; Bettmann 12; Bernard Cahier 11; Paul-Henri Cahier 72; Michael Cooper/Allsport 95; Daily Express Hulton Archive 24; Jerome Delay/AFP 88; Fred Enke/The Enthusiast Network 30; Evening Standard/Hulton Archive 15; GP Library/Universal Images Group 16, 77; Kym Illman 122; Toshifumi Kitamura/AFP 57; John Lamm/The Enthusiast Network 31; Martyn Lucy 155; Clive Mason 119; National Motor Museum/Heritage Images 89; David Phipps/Sutton Images 19, 32, 38, 39, 41, 43, 64, 67, 86-87; Pascal Rondeau/Allsport 58, 74-75; Mark Thompson 80; Jean-Marc Zaorski/Gamma-Rapho 59; Hoch Zwei/Corbis 117

MOTORSPORT IMAGES: 13, 23, 25, 28, 42, 50-51, 66, 71, 84; Ercole Colombo 54, 78; Glenn Dunbar 116; Andy Hone 81; LAT 49, 91, 92, 146; Zak Mauger 134; Rainer Schlegelmilch 8, 20-21, 52, 90; Sutton Images 37, 53, 60, 69, 145; Steven Tee/LAT 99

SHUTTERSTOCK: 115, 150-151; Eric Alonso/DPPI 138, 139; Diego Azubel/EPA 109, 113; Xavi Bonilla/DPPI 136-137; Colorsport 34-35; Carl Court/EPA 112; DPPI 4; Alejandro Garcia/EPA 125; Felix Heyder/EPA 104; Martin Keep/ProSports 130; Adolf Martinez Soler 142; Gerry Penny/EPA 98; Pixathlon 126-127; F Schneider/imageBROKER 148; Sipa 61, 106, 110; Antonin Vincent/DPPI 135; Valdrin Xhemaj/EPA-EFE 129

Every effort has been made to acknowledge correctly and contact the source and/or copyright holder of each picture. Any unintentional errors or omissions will be corrected in future editions of this book.